# BEATING THE MIDAS CURSE

# *Beating* the

# MIDAS CUR$E

### SECOND EDITION

*by*

## Perry L. Cochell & Rod Zeeb

A

PUBLICATION

Second Edition November 2013
First Edition November 2005
ISBN 978-1494735456

Senior Editor: Brad Haga
Associate Editor: Kate E. Stephenson

Printed in the USA

GenUs LLC
701 North Green Valley Parkway, Suite 200,
Henderson, Nevada, 89074
*info@genusu.com*

*Family first*

# ACKNOWLEDGEMENTS

We would like to thank The Heritage Institute staff for all of their help with this endeavor over the years, with special thanks to Ryan Zeeb, Brian Bell, Lori Coonen and Susan Wise. We also want to thank the contributors to the first edition of this book for their help and insights and all of the rest of the members of The Heritage Institute for their support. And, special thanks to Richard and Sibylle Beck, G.M. "Milt" and Marilyn Butler, Dave and Marcia Lantz, Stan and Donna Zeeb and Clay and Elinor Zeeb for helping to make The Heritage Institute possible.

## Rod
My special thanks to Robert Esperti, who introduced me to the concepts of multigenerational and values-based planning; to my brother, Rick Zeeb, who helped me meld the principles of Heritage Design with current financial planning; to Monica Estabrooke for her passion for philanthropy and her insights into integrating these principles with charities; to Susan Wise, Lori Coonen, Ken Stoner and others who helped me work with so many families since 1989; and to the many attorneys, CPAs, financial advisors and nonprofits who have allowed me to work with their clients and donors. And, a very special thank you to my children, Christina and Ryan, who have helped me focus my values and have provided pure joy in my life.

## Perry
In memory of my loving mother, Wanda Darlene Cochell.

## Perry and Rod
Our gratitude is endless to the clients, friends and others who have trusted us with assisting them in passing on their values to future generations. Finally, both Perry and Rod thank Brad Haga for his encouragement and support with this book. We would not have taken on this project without his encouragement and expertise.

*A note about the cover design*

The 1st edition of this book, published in 2005, featured three gold-plated apples on the cover. As with the cover of this 2nd edition, the descending size of the apples from large to small symbolized the loss of wealth and unity that so many families experience from one generation to the next.

Using gold apples on the 1st cover design reflected the significance that the authors placed on making sure that affluent families in particular learned about the dangers that the *Midas Curse* posed to their families and their fortunes.

In the eight years since the 1st edition was published, though, the authors have seen time and again that the devastating effects of the *Midas Curse* fall equally upon individuals and families at all income levels.

Therefore, the principles and solutions presented in this new edition offer *every* family the opportunity to become stronger and more unified today, and to remain that way for generations.

That is why we (carefully!) washed the gold-plating off the apples on the cover of the 1st edition, and replaced them here with three bright red, all natural, good-for-everybody apples.

Yes, the *Midas Curse* can affect any family. The good news, however, is that any family can now arm themselves with the knowledge necessary to defeat the *Midas Curse* and prosper for generations to come.

An apple a day, after all......

# TABLE OF CONTENTS

# FOREWORD

*Heritage design*, which is the subject of this book, is a relatively new approach to planning for the things that matter most to us. Heritage design helps people to go well beyond planning for the (postmortem) distribution of the assets they have accumulated in their lives. It helps them to identify and share what they care most deeply about, to understand how their real legacy will affect their inheritors, and it guides them in a process that defines the true legacy they want to leave. Most importantly, heritage design helps people to begin working with their family members *right now* to achieve the current and future outcomes that matter the most to them, for reasons that they identify and articulate for themselves.

Here is how heritage design fits into the planning continuum:

Successful Multi-Generational Planning is a 3-Part Process

**FINANCIAL PLANNING**
*Protects and Grows Your Money*

**HERITAGE DESIGN**
*Prepares Your Family for Their Inheritance*

**ESTATE PLANNING**
*Prepares Your Money for Your Family*

To help illustrate the impact of heritage design we will provide comparisons between the multi-generational outcomes that families who exclusively rely upon traditional planning experience, and the outcomes experienced by families who (formally or informally) make heritage design the foundation for their planning.

As you read these real-world stories, we hope that you will think about what you would like to see happening inside your own family today, and for generations to come.

Financial and Estate planning pass *what you own*
to future generations.

Heritage Design passes
*who you are.*

# INTRODUCTION

The architect's father had a terminal illness, and at best, a few years to live. He had built an estate worth over twelve million dollars but had not completed his estate planning. The minute the doctor gave him the long face his procrastination was over, and the architect was at the advisor's office to fast track his parents' estate plan.

His mother and father knew exactly how they wanted their estate to be distributed. They had five children; three daughters, two sons (including the architect), and eighteen grandchildren. The sons had been successful, and each was financially independent. For the daughters, however, life had been one struggle after another; each had been married and divorced, two of them were battling substance issues, and all of them were strapped financially.

To help their daughters, the parents had recently purchased each of them a new home—fully paid for. In their updated estate planning the parents now directed that a significant amount of their wealth be transferred to the daughters and the daughters' children so that they would be financially secure after the parents passed on. For the sons, the parents instructed that trusts be created that would be accessible when they retired.

The architect conveyed his parents' sense of urgency to have their wishes translated into all of the necessary estate documents as quickly as possible. The elderly couple's wishes were clear, there were no complex legal or financial structures in place to slow the final planning process, so the estate planning documents came together quickly.

Instruments were drafted to transfer a significant amount of money to the daughters, and tax-favorable trusts were created that would be paid to the sons in the future. From a purely legal and financial perspective, the estate plan constructed for the architect's parents was well conceived, carefully crafted, and it complied with the highest national standards. It was, in fact, a textbook application of the best traditional estate planning practices available.

Still, as the poet Robert Burns reminds us, *"The best laid plans of mice and men often go awry..."* One week to the day after the planning was complete, the architect called with news of a death in his family. However, it was his mother, not his father, who had unexpectedly died. And there was more: six days after her death, his grieving father passed away. This estate plan had come full circle, from planning to implementation, in just a few weeks.

As planned, the estate's assets were subjected to minimal taxation. The money the parents wanted to make available immediately for the daughters was transferred to them, and the trusts established for future distribution to the sons were securely in place.

To be honest, there was no small amount of satisfaction (OK, pride!) on the part of the advisor who authored the plan; everything that could be done to help this family minimize taxes and to pass the wealth to the children had been done—and in record time. This was what being an estate-planning attorney was all about, he thought.

, , ,

Two years later, the architect returned to the advisor's office with a heartbreaking story of what had transpired after the distribution of his parents' assets. The family was being torn apart. His three sisters were once again in deep financial trouble. Each had spent her share of the inheritance. Every penny. All three homes, gifts from the parents, had been mortgaged to the hilt. And now, the architect said, the sisters were demanding that he and his brother tap their own inheritance trusts to help them, because it was "what mom and dad would want them to do." But how could he? He knew that any money they were given would quickly evaporate. Their spending has always been out of control, he said. What happened, he wanted to know? What should he do?

The best laid plans, indeed.

It took just twenty-four months for the daughters to blow through most of the assets that their parents had worked for half a century to acquire. The architect's family was being destroyed, and there wasn't a legal or accounting solution in the world that could stitch it back together. Worst of all, the family unity and harmony that all parents hope their children will enjoy lay in ruins. In a very real sense, all of that money and all of those carefully crafted asset transfer plans and tax reduction strategies had been reduced to rubble.

And yet, the advisor knew that it was not the planning that had failed. Objectively speaking it accomplished exactly what it was designed to do: transfer the greatest amount of assets with the smallest tax liability possible to the heirs. By any generally accepted legal or financial standards, by any objective definition of a "successful" plan, this one was a gold plated winner. The operation was a complete success. Pity that the patient died, of course.

, , ,

It is impossible to envision any scenario in which the parents would willfully set out to plan a final legacy that included a broken family and a squandered fortune. In fact, advisors across the professional spectrum agree that whatever their clients' individual approaches to estate planning may be, there are four desired outcomes that matter most to people:

> 1. They want to protect their family from ever being destitute.
> 2. They want to provide their family with opportunities that will help them mature into healthy, productive adults.
> 3. They do not want to promote a non-working lifestyle. As investor Warren Buffett said, "The perfect inheritance is enough money so that they would feel they could do anything, but not so much that they could do nothing."1

> 4. They want to create a culture of communication and harmony in their family.

These are deeply significant objectives. They are expressions of both heart and mind. No sophisticated legal or financial mumbo-jumbo is required to understand why people identify the achievement of those four outcomes as their most important planning objectives.

They just make sense.

But for the advisor who had so carefully structured the detailed plans for the architect's parents, the "after-shocks" that were tearing the family apart raised a troubling question: where in his professional education or practice, where in the binders stuffed to bursting with contracts, trust structures and contingency codicils, where in the practice management libraries or accounting and legal reference documents were the tools that he could have applied to help his clients actually achieve what mattered most to them?

He knew that traditional financial and estate planning are concerned with one thing and one thing only: growing and transferring the assets. Traditional planning asks, "*Who gets the money that's left over after taxes, legal fees and administrative costs are paid?*" But the architect's advisor knew that for people who regarded multigenerational family unity and individual family member productivity and achievement as being every bit as important as maintaining the family wealth, planners needed to begin asking even more important questions:

"How can we design structures and plans that will help to pass on the family's true wealth: its traditions, values, stories, life lessons and experiences? And how can we help to manage the material wealth of the family so that it is becomes a tool to secure what matters most to them for generations to come?"

, , ,

Traditional planning counts the assets, and divides and distributes the "spoils" according to the language of the Will. Over the centuries the practices and policies of traditional financial and estate planning have been developed, refined, shaped re-shaped over and over. Engaging in such planning constitute a ubiquitous rite of passage for each of us who step into a professional advisor's office to "get our things in order." When someone tells us "I've done my planning," we know what they mean: they have gone through a time-honored process of measuring, weighing and planning for the doling out of the "stuff" they have accumulated over a lifetime. In fact, as you will discover in this book, the only thing more commonplace than our blanket acceptance of and reliance upon the much-honored practice of traditional financial and estate planning is this one small fact: traditional financial and estate planning fail. Not occasionally. Not now and again. *They almost always fail.* And they have failed for as long as historical records have been kept.

, , ,

We have worked with thousands of people, from mid-income business owners and professionals to dozens of the wealthiest families in America. In our years of combined experience and research, we have seen too many good plans disintegrate the moment the assets began to flow through the fingers of unprepared heirs.

We routinely see children who do not understand what it took for their parents to accumulate their wealth, and who were never taught a proper relationship with money. Children who were not aware that their family's wealth, like most affluent people's, consists of just two things: real estate and securities—not cash. ("OK, but now show me the *real* money," are among the most common words attorneys hear during the estate settlement process.)

We have seen families ripped to shreds as they battle over money. And—most tragically from our perspectives not just as attorneys, but as parents ourselves—we have seen too many children who never learned that the most important inheritance their parents left to them had nothing whatsoever to do with money.

Sadly, the reality of family chaos and destruction are not the exception to the rule following the implementation of the estate planning. Ask any advisor who works within the estate planning arena how often they see client families thrown into turmoil and the family assets lost because the money—not the family—was the focus of the planning. Be forewarned— you'll want to hold onto your hat when the advisor answers. (Which we will do ourselves shortly.)

Over time we concluded that families are not adequately served by the traditional estate planning system. The idea that the transfer of assets and the promotion of tax savings are the most important legacy that one generation should strive to pass to the next was simply not a proposition we could support.

That is not, by any means, a criticism of advisors who construct traditional plans on behalf of their clients. They do their jobs (which to be honest we should call "death planning," not estate planning) well, particularly when you consider the constraints placed upon them by tradition, practice, and even by the law. The specific responsibility of the traditional advisor is to transfer assets and to reduce taxes, after all, not to "save" families. However, we *did* want to help save families. Towards that end we worked individually and in concert over two decades to develop *The Heritage Process,*™ which is our own comprehensive application of heritage design. This process represents one of the most significant shifts in thinking in the field of financial and estate planning since the sixteenth century. Thousands of people have experienced the *"family first, fortune second"* perspective of this process. They have discovered that by putting their values ahead of their valuables when they plan, they greatly increase the chances of securing them both, for generations to come.

Our individual and combined experience, observation and practice as we developed *The Heritage Process*™ led us to make two significant conclusions about money and families:

1. We believe that the tide of family destruction caused by money *can be resolved,* and its effects even reversed.

2. We believe that traditional planning advisors can work as partners with what has come to be known as *heritage design* to construct living plans that can strengthen the family right now and across generations in ways that no will, trust, or bank account can ever do.

Finally, this note: the underlying premise of heritage design is that the values by which you live are your most important asset, and the greatest inheritance you will leave to your children. Successful planning has nothing to do with affluence. It's not about the money. It's about your family.

*Perry Cochell & Rod Zeeb*
November, 2013

# THE 90% WORLD

I magine living in a world where the probability that you're going to take a tumble the minute you get out of bed is a whopping 90%. A world where there is a 9 out of 10 chance that there will be no hot water when you step into the shower. And then, 90% odds that your spouse will say, *"Sorry honey, no food in the fridge, you'll have to grab something on the way to the office."* Which by the way, will be pretty unlikely given the overwhelming odds that your car won't start when you turn the ignition.

That may not be such a bad thing, of course, since those pesky odds would follow you out the driveway and make you a shoo-in to be involved in a car accident once you were finally on the road. As for your chances of walking away from that one… in our 90% world Las Vegas won't be taking any bets on you going dancing this weekend.

A 90% probability of *anything* happening pretty much constitutes an actuarial certainty.

Fortunately, in the real world, our chances of having to stare doom in the face on a daily basis are pretty limited. The odds of being struck by lightning sometime in your life are 1 in 3,000. Of being attacked by a shark, about 1 in 700,000. As for winning the big lottery, let's just agree that isn't in the cards in any world, 90% or not.

Still, those are odds we can—and do—live with. It goes against human nature to suggest that any of us would set out to get married, build a house, start a business, have children or do anything else important knowing there was a 90% chance that we'd fail.

Consider, however, the process and products that make up traditional estate planning. If there is one area of your life where you really want to hit the bulls-eye, it's here. We try to share our dreams, our hopes, and our most important values with those we love while we are alive, but we also have an instinctive desire to provide for our families after we're gone. That's what we *hope* we can accomplish through the estate planning process.

Plus, many of us want to leave a legacy that passes not just money to our family, but that also passes *meaning*, the essential significance of the life we lived. And, we want to know that our lives meant something, that in our passage through this world we made a difference. Psychologists explain this idea by telling us that it is not really death that we fear so much. Instead, what we really fear is insignificance, the idea that at the end of the day our lives didn't amount to all that much. That we didn't set ripples in motion in the lives of our families, friends and neighbors that would carry our accomplishments and our values on after we are gone.

The human desire to leave a significant legacy is extremely powerful. Across the centuries people have expended enormous energy and resources to develop mechanisms by which they could protect and pass on their valuables to their heirs.

Whether the estate is that of a pauper or a prince, the driving force behind estate planning has always been to provide for the future, to ensure that your loved ones will have basic necessities like homes, medical care, and education.

Each of us will leave a legacy of some sort, whether we plan for it or not, whether we have children or not. The poet and the artist leave ideas and images to future generations. Working people may leave a home, and some insurance. The self-employed businessman may leave factories, investment portfolios, and complex trusts. No matter what you have accomplished in life, or how much or how little you have accumulated, one thing is certain: *Whether by choice or by chance, you will leave something behind.*

Or, as our friend from Texas, Dan Garrett likes to say: *"Even if you only own two suits when you die, they are only going to bury you in one, so one will pass to someone."*

⸻

Now, the bad news. The overwhelming odds are that what you really want to leave your family probably won't be anything like what they will actually receive, no matter how extensive and carefully crafted your planning may be. That is because in 9 out of 10 cases the things that a family truly needs to receive from the parents if they are going to be able to thrive and prosper across the years *won't even be mentioned during the estate planning process.*

Why not? Because there really is an upside-down world where a 90% failure rate is the norm. This world has existed for millennia. And, dominated by the combined forces of inertia and tradition, that world and its 90% failure rate goes strong to this day. It has been a reality of the financial and estate planning communities for centuries.

It is accepted without question from the boardrooms of Fortune 500 companies to the ivory towers of academia. Because of it, relationships will be broken, families will be destroyed, businesses will be devastated, and fortunes will be lost.

Ask an auditorium filled with financial planners and estate planning attorneys if this world exists and you will see every head nod in agreement. Add to that our own experiences with clients and families across the years, our research of financial, legal and historical documents and our interviews and interactions with professional colleagues in several disciplines, and the conclusion that we reached relative to the research, teaching and work that we do on behalf of families becomes inescapable:

**90% of all traditional inheritance plans will fail.**

In part, this conclusion is based on numerous studies that conclude that in families where new wealth has been created by the first generation, 7 out of 10 of those families' fortunes will be gone by the end of the second generation. By the end of the third generation,

9 out of the 10 families will be broke. (This statistic was recently referenced in a March 7, 2013 Wall Street Journal article titled *"Lost Inheritances"*.)

This book was born out of the impact that conclusion has had upon us both professionally and personally. It is why The Heritage Institute was founded, and why we created *The Heritage Process,*™ which has become the best known form of heritage design in the nation.

Our work is founded upon a simple premise: we believe that when parents who build wealth pass only their *material assets* to their children, and not the values by which they have lived, there is little chance that the family, or its wealth, will survive for long.

That is not to say that we dismiss the products or process of traditional estate planning outright; on the contrary, investments, trusts and other financial and legal instruments are, and always will be, the vehicle for the transmission of the *things* a family owns. But money is just a tool, as likely to separate families as it is to unify them. Your financial net worth is a statistic, not a legacy. To appreciate that fact is to understand that your family cannot be defined in terms of the things you *own*; real estate valuations, spreadsheets, trust documents and bank account balances describe a *condition*, not a family. You and your children, your grandchildren and generations of your family yet unborn, can only be defined by the values, stories, experiences and traditions which have shaped your unique family history for many years.

What, then, is a legacy by the terms of our definition? If material assets are not the most important things we leave behind, what is? Also, how do we go about shaping such a "non-material" legacy and communicating it to those we love? These questions have been the focus of our research and work for many years.

We have learned that if families place their *valuables* ahead of their *values* when they do their planning they will probably end up with neither. That supports our conclusion that the most important inheritance that your children will ever receive from you will come while you are still alive, not after you are gone. It is an inheritance that won't be found at your bank, or inside your stock portfolio.

That's because your most valuable asset is embedded in the fabric of your everyday life. It is constructed from the values you learned from important people in your own life. It is something that you live and model day in and day out to your family, friends, co-workers, and to the community of people and organizations who make up your world.

If your priorities during life are your family and your values, you should maintain those priorities with death (estate) planning. That means making sure that the financial inheritance you leave will be used not as a piggy-bank, but as a tool and a resource to support the things that you and your family agree matter the most to you as individuals and as a family.

The traditional estate planning process that has been the norm for centuries has focused on money (get more) and taxes (pay less), rather than on family and values (at all). Now that we know that traditional planning fails in its primary mission of keeping the money in the family 90% of the time, don't you agree that it is time for advisors, clients, families and lawmakers to do something about it?

, , ,

Heritage design puts family before fortune in the planning process. In doing so, the chances that the family can thrive in its relationships and still prosper materially for generations are greatly enhanced. That is not an assumption. It is fact.

Families who construct their planning on a heritage design foundation achieve a better understanding of their relationship to wealth, and to one another. They learn to communicate more clearly and more honestly about things like money and philanthropy, as well as about their shared goals and objectives. They learn—by doing, not just by talking—how to make the money a tool to achieve the most important goals of all—family unity and individual achievement. They listen to stories about the hardships and triumphs that brought the family to where it is today, and they talk openly and from the heart about deeply important matters, like the sustaining quality of faith.

Rod recalls a conversation he once had with a client about the heritage design process. The hard-charging, no-nonsense Type A client had built a billion-dollar business from the ground-up. To be more precise, he built his business empire from the inside of a used '59 Ford pickup that had an apple crate bolted to the floor for the passenger seat.

"Sounds like the soft side of planning to me," said the tough CEO after Rod explained what heritage design was all about. "Don't know that I much care for that kind of touchy-feely stuff. It would be pretty hard to quantify things like tradition and stories in a spreadsheet."

Rod chuckled. "So let me ask you: how soft is your love for your children and grandchildren? How soft is your love for your business, and the 1,200 employees who depend on it to take care of their families? History says that everything you have spent the last 50 years building is going to begin to die about the time that you do. That sound soft?"

At this writing the business-owner and his family have been engaged in heritage design for over a decade.

Traditional planning has failed too many families. Heritage design is for all families—not just the affluent. Its guiding rules and principles just make sense. It does not adhere to a rigid set of hard and fast rules; it is built on general principles that anyone can understand. The tools to strengthen and unify your family across generations are already in your possession. With those tools, you can begin to turn the 90% world on its head.

You *can* pass both your values and your valuables to future generations.

Do you know your great-grandmother's first name?

Do you know what she stood for, what she believed in, and what she fought for?

Do you want *your* great-grandchildren to know your first name, and what mattered most to you?

, , ,

## THE STORY OF KING MIDAS

Some people who pick this book up for the first time will rack their brain to recall the story of King Midas, whose mythical affliction was the inspiration for the title of this book.

You may recall the ancient Greek legend...

Midas was a kind man and benevolent King, blessed with financial abundance. He had a beautiful palace with extensive gardens in which he loved to walk. He loved animals and kept favorite pets. The apple of his eye was his beautiful daughter; just hearing her laugh brought him joy. And he had a tremendous amount of wealth, mostly in bars and bags of gold.

Midas loved gold. He would go into his royal treasury and gaze at it for hours on end. He loved the way it shone, the noise it made when he would throw coins up in the air and let them shower down over his head. He liked the smoothness of it in his hand. He loved to earn it, count it and hoard it. Midas was a happy man.

One day he came upon old Silenus, a friend of the god Dionysus, wandering lost in the forest. Midas took Silenus home and cared for him for eleven days. When Dionysus finally found his friend, he was so grateful for Midas's kindness that he granted him one wish. Against the advice of the god, Midas asked that everything he touch turn to gold. When he woke the next morning, he tentatively touched the table next to his bed. It instantly turned to gold. Midas leaped up, and laughing and dancing began touching everything in sight: the floors, the walls, the draperies, the furniture.

He ran through the palace grounds touching tables, statues, paintings, trees, and even the palace gates.

He was delirious with joy! In one instant, all of his dreams had come true. Piles of pure gold, glorious and perfect, sent from heaven—and it was all his with only a simple, effortless touch! No work, no sacrifice, no planning. He had realized his deepest desire. He was rich, rich beyond calculation, and there was no end to how much he could possess. Surely, he was the most blessed of men.

Out of breath, he stopped to walk through his beloved garden and picked a rose to smell. By the time he brought it to his nose, it was lifeless metal. Midas paused. He would have to be careful from now on and just bend over a flower to sniff it. Exhausted and hungry, he decided to have a meal. But by the time he put a grape in his mouth it had turned hard and cold. He nearly choked on wine that turned to liquid gold in his throat.

His favorite cat jumped onto his lap and suddenly, instead of the soft fur he loved, there was only a cold statue. Midas began to cry in despair as he realized what he had done. His beloved daughter, hearing his distress, ran to comfort him with a hug; and before he could stop her she, too, was transformed. Midas was heartbroken. Truly repentant now, he begged Dionysus to take away his curse. Knowing that he had learned his lesson, Dionysus told Midas what he must do.

"First, you must wash your hands in the river. Then bring jugs of water from the river, and pour them over the things you changed. Second, you must give away all of your wealth."

Midas promised. He followed the god's instructions and soon his beautiful daughter was restored to him. Hearing her laugh again brought him to tears. King Midas gave all of his wealth to the poor, and moved to a small cabin in the woods, where he and his beloved daughter lived out their days in complete happiness.

، ، ،

The story of King Midas is not just a cautionary tale about greed, or a warning to be careful for what you wish. It is an enduring reminder of the things in life from which true happiness springs.

Traditional estate planning with its assets-only focus, misses those things. Wills, trusts, stocks, real estate deeds—even money itself—are just pieces of paper. King Midas discovered that real happiness could be achieved only if he put love for family before love for fortune.

This book is dedicated to that ideal.

# CHAPTER ONE

## The Fire

The October night is clear and cool. Smoke drifts from a few chimneys in the wooded neighborhood, thinning to whispers before disappearing behind the full yellow moon. Piles of orange and brown leaves line the sidewalks, and here and there a lonely rake rests against a tree in anticipation of the final autumn clean up.

At the end of the cul-de-sac a two-story Victorian home is framed by a big leaf maple and a towering blue spruce. A basketball hoop is mounted above the garage door, and two bikes lean against a woodshed that is piled high with cords of seasoned oak and Douglas fir.

Suddenly, the sound of a single bark breaks the evening calm as Max lifts his head from between his paws to warn away a pilfering squirrel. The tiny animal races away from his perch beside the dog house to the safety of a bush bordering the daylight basement window.

Sunrise will bring another day of work and school and play in a few hours. For the moment, Max and most of those in his world are at rest. The squirrel is also ready for sleep, but a sudden burst of light from the basement window sends it skittering across the yard, up the fence and into the dependable safety of the maple tree.

The basement windows are splashed with light the instant a pile of varnish-soaked rags ignite beside the gas water heater. Flames gnaw at the antique library table that Jack was re-finishing earlier in the day, and then they jump to an overhanging shelf lined with open cans of turpentine and shellac.

The fire begins to feel its strength, twisting and curling its fingers upward in search of more fuel. It feeds on everything: paint cans, old books, folded cotton clothing. Then, it wraps up around the stairs, and, with a ferocious surge, leaps to the exposed joists in the basement ceiling above. The basement is engulfed in fire, and as smoke begins to fan up into the house through the furnace vents, the hallway smoke alarm shrieks to life.

, , ,

Jack wakes, and immediately shakes his wife out of her deep sleep. As they clamber out of bed, they can smell the thick, varnish-laden smoke. They know that they have only a minute to get the kids out of the house to safety.

It only takes a moment to pull their frightened children from bed, to race down the stairs through the billowing smoke then out the front door into the moonlit yard. As Jack pulls his wife and children outside to safety, he sees red-orange flames materialize at the back of the house. Super-heated smoke swirls upward with brutal intensity. At that moment he realizes that if the fire is still confined to the kitchen and back bath, he might have time to go back inside. Only a minute, maybe forty or fifty seconds, but still, time to grab something. Enough time to get a few important things before the fire guts the house.

But...to get what? What should he take? Jack hesitates in the entryway. His briefcase and laptop computer are down the hallway in his home office. Easy to get to. Important, too, especially since much of his original research data and notes haven't been backed up. There'd be hell to pay at work if he set this project back by a couple of months.

He knows he has only a moment to decide what to grab, just what he and his family absolutely need. All that information...finances, business, taxes and insurance...a nightmare to have to rebuild.

The fire is roaring now, and the heat slams against him like a desert wind. He can hear sirens in the distance at the same instant that windows in the kitchen begin to pop and explode as the fire pushes relentlessly against the walls in search of more oxygen.

Jack starts down the hallway, coughing against the acrid smoke that rolls across the ceiling like gray ocean waves. The fire must have started in the basement, he thinks, the wooden floor is searing hot beneath his bare feet.

As he races towards the office door, he suddenly feels as if he is being watched. In a way he is. Five generations of family line the walls: from the 1847 tintypes of his wife's great-great grandparents, to WWII pictures of handsome young men in uniform, wedding and christening photos, picnics and family reunions.... the birth of his children.

He only has a second to look, but in that instant he sees more than he had noticed in the thousands of trips he had made down the hall over the past ten years. Ten years in this house. Ten years of walking through his family history every morning and every night. Why hasn't he made copies? No time to worry about that now. The heat is fierce, and it is getting harder to see through the smoke. There is time to get one good arm load; he has to get out!

The sirens are so loud now they sound like they are in his garage. That's good, he thinks, the fire department is here. His wife and kids will be fine. He'll be OK, too. Just grab as much as he can. One load. He takes two more steps down the hall, and turns into his office. The room is bathed in a smoky orange glow—just enough to see by.

, , ,

What to take? There are the banker's boxes, bulging with years' worth of financial records. On the desk, his laptop screen glows softly, beckoning with files of data that had taken two months to research and develop. And in the filing cabinet, so many records, so much stuff….and then, he remembers the silver! His wife's silver plate and cutlery. Collecting heirloom silver is her passion, and a considerable investment, to boot. Will it survive the heat of the inferno if he leaves it in the house? Will they be able to find any of it in the ashes after the fire is extinguished? How hot does it have to get before silver melts….and how much can he carry, anyway?

Wait a minute. What about their personal financial records in the two bankers' boxes in the closet? Years' worth, and all critical for taxes and planning. Plus, his life insurance paper. Why hadn't he purchased a fire proof safe? He'd thought about it so many times. Where were they, oh yes, in a shoe box next to the filing cabinet. Weren't the trust deed documents in there, too, and all the rest of his bank records?

His kids' report cards and their birth certificates. Passports, too. It had only been about fifteen seconds since he ran back into the house, but it seemed he had been there for an eternity. The heat is suffocating now, the smoke is thick, black and greasy. All right, time to decide. Take it, don't look back, and don't regret the choice. There was so much they would need, so many documents and records upon which they depended. Then a crash, and sounds of wood splitting as the kitchen floor caves in, and a great whooshing noise as the blaze from the basement surges up into the house.

That was it. Jack makes his decision. He fills his arms until he can barely see over the load, and runs as fast as he can down the smoky hallway, out onto the porch, and into the sweet, clear night air. His wife and children are under the maple tree, shivering in their pajamas. Max stands at attention in front of them; whatever is going on isn't going to get past him to hurt his family.

Several neighbors are already there comforting the children. A police cruiser and two fire trucks race up to the curb, firefighters hit the ground and run towards the fully engulfed house before their trucks come to a complete stop.

Jack lurches towards his wife, the load in his arms about to fall. She sees him, and grateful tears well in her eyes; her family is safe. That's all that matters right now.

, , ,

And then she sees what he has gathered in his arms, the things he risked his life to save as their home—everything they had accumulated—was burning down around him. She rushes to help him and embrace him, and her tears turn to deep sobs.

She takes as much as she can from his arms and then turns back to her children. She sees the fire hoses come to life and hears the urgency in the Chief's voice as he shouts to his men to attack the flames that crackle above the house, shooting thousands of glowing embers into the starry night. She looks again at what her husband carried through the fire. The only things she has to begin building their new home.

And she smiles.

# If it was your house?
*A brief exercise*

## ~~THE~~ *YOUR* FIRE

Imagine that it is your own home that is burning, and that, like Jack, your family is safely outside. You have less than a minute to grab something(s) of importance to you and your family.

Please think about these questions. If you're doing this exercise with a spouse, friend or other family member, write your answers down privately and then compare them. Sharing your honest answers is half the fun, so, don't give them any hints.

1. What do you think Jack chose to carry out with him? Why did you come to that conclusion?

2. What would you take? Why?

3. Was it a difficult decision to make?

4. Was your decision based more on a personal value, or on a sense of the financial or material importance of what you chose?

After you have completed this thought exercise, share your answers with your spouse or another person who has read the chapter about the fire. Did you make the same choices? For the same reasons?

# CHAPTER TWO

## In Tradition We Trust?

*"Every object in a state of uniform motion tends to remain in that state of motion unless an external force is applied to it."* Sir Isaac Newton

We regularly address the men and women who plan for and manage the money of the most affluent Americans. They include estate planning attorneys, financial planners, CPAs and planned-giving officers for non-profits. These professionals are the best in their fields. When they walk in the door for the first day of an intensive three-day academy called *Counseling the Affluent,* they bring with them years of practical, hands-on experience dealing with some of the nation's wealthiest families and individuals.

Their clients encompass every ethnic, religious and cultural background, with net worths ranging from a few million to several billion dollars (and change). Their backgrounds vary, from manufacturers and physicians, to real estate developers, Fortune 500

CEOs, athletes and actors, even the occasional "dot-commer."

No two of these advisors' clients are quite alike, and no two of their financial or estate plans will look the same.

But, as we look out over the audience, we know there is at least one "tradition" that several client families of every advisor in the group have shared.

"Let me ask for a show of hands," Perry will say. "How many of you have personally seen client families that have been destroyed in one way or another as a direct result of their affluence?" Hands shoot up instantly. All of them. At every presentation.

"How many of you have seen an estate built by a client with hard work and sacrifice over many years blown away by his or her children and grandchildren?" Again, raised hands fill the meeting room.

"Now," continues Rod, " how many of you think the parents or grandparents who spent their lives building the family wealth planned for that to happen?"

For the first time, no hands are raised.

Around the room, the advisors to affluent families exchange knowing glances. They've seen the eighteen-year old get a million dollars cash, with no strings attached courtesy of granddad's will. Followed immediately by the hot car, the cocaine, the parties, and finally rehab, jail, or even suicide. They've seen marriages break up, friendships devastated and family members alienated from each other.

They've watched the companies that grandparents and parents sweated and sacrificed for decades to build go under, as heirs eager to squeeze more cash from the estate broke them up, sold them at bargain prices, or lost them through mismanagement. From a legal, technical and "state-of-the-art" traditional planning perspective, the advisors to the families going through these problems followed prudent, conservative and generally accepted standards and practices as they crafted their clients' financial and estate plans.

They diligently planned for the future of client valuables. They sought out every legal deduction, capitalized on the latest federal rulings relative to investments and trusts, and crafted complex instruments to minimize estate taxes. They followed tradition.

Sadly, so did many of the heirs.

, , ,

The unfortunate historical "tradition" of the collapse of family wealth across several generations is not news to your financial or legal advisors. It wasn't news two thousand years ago when a Chinese scholar penned the adage: *"fu bu guo san dai,"* or "Wealth never survives three generations." Nor was it a surprise in thirteenth century England, where the proverb, "Clogs to clogs in three generations," which morphed by the 1600s to *"Rags to riches to rags."* In nineteenth century America, where fortunes were made and lost with astounding speed amidst the gold fields, oil wells, copper mines and railroad booms, people said "From shirtsleeves to shirtsleeves in *three generations."*

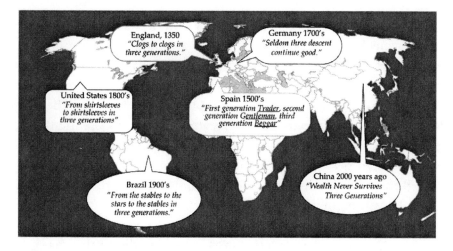

Many cultures. Thousands of years of history. One common tradition of failure.

Adam Smith summed it up over two hundred years ago in his landmark book *The Wealth of Nations.* "Riches, in spite of the most violent regulations of law to prevent their dissipation, very seldom remain long in the same family."

How did these traditions evolve? And, why do we continue them? To get some perspective, let's take a trip to the bank...

The marble porticos, heroic statues and Georgian façade of the

Bank of England's central office on Threadneedle Street in London are among the best known architectural features in the world. As you walk through the massive bronze entry and past the liveried doorman, you might get a sense that very little has changed since King William and Queen Mary created the bank in 1694.

And you'd be right—in more ways than you might think. The bank was created because the public finances of England were weak, and the system of money and credit was in disarray. With a loan of a million pounds from one of the nation's wealthiest men, the new national bank was founded. In just a few short years, the practices and traditions of the Bank of England became a model for the world.

, , ,

Today, customers can make deposits or withdrawals, open and manage checking accounts, apply for loans, purchase government-backed bonds, get investment portfolio advice, plan for retirement or meet with their private bank officer. One stop financial planning and money management. Of course, in September, 1734, when the Bank of England moved into its present location, the very same menu of services was available to customers. Except for the ruffled clothing and powdered wigs, a customer from the year 2006 would find almost everything in the great institution of nearly three centuries ago to be very familiar.

The motto of bankers worldwide since the fourteenth century has been "Let the money do the work." It is a tradition they have followed scrupulously through wars and depressions, boom times and bust. What is extraordinary is that in their combined roles as repository, guardian and manager of our money, banks at the dawn of the twenty-first century are really so similar to those of five hundred years ago.

Of course, they accomplish the movement of money and information at a much faster pace, and, sad but true, you were not given a toaster when you opened a savings account in the 1800s.

The banking industry has long occupied a central role in estate planning. For many people, banks are *the* key player in the process, as they perform vital trust management, investment guidance and other financial services relative to the establishment, maintenance, and ultimate disposition of estate assets. If we were to travel back in time four thousand years to ancient Egypt to attend the public reading of a last will and testament, the proceedings would look a lot like they do today (well, except for the chariots outside the attorney's office). The products and services offered by the most modern banks to globe-trotting businessmen are nearly identical to what a wool merchant from the Scottish Highlands could find when he climbed out of a hansom cab at the steps of the Bank of England three hundred years ago. Sir Isaac Newton would call that inertia. We could just as easily call it tradition.

Tradition is a powerful concept. It reminds us of our duty to family, community, country and faith. It provides a framework for our routines and rituals, from weddings and funerals to our daily conduct of business. It provides important cultural and historical cohesion. However, when it comes to examining the role that tradition plays in financial planning, and in particular estate planning, there's a flip side of the tradition "coin" at which we should be looking.

That's the side that shows the *Titanic* ramming the iceberg. Icebergs were hardly unknown at the time. But, the great ship's designers and engineers were certain that the *Titanic* was unsinkable. After all, hadn't they had planned it that way? Unsinkable planning is no more achievable than an unsinkable luxury liner—no matter what the First Class staterooms (planning fees) may cost.

Traditional planning is potentially hazardous because it only addresses the visible part of the iceberg—your money—and ignores all of what lies hidden beneath the surface: your hopes and dreams, your values, life lessons and experiences, and especially, your family.

As Mark Twain noted, tradition should be our guide—not our jailer. We should, as individuals, as families, as professionals and as lawmakers, re-examine the institutions and practices that have guided estate planning for hundreds of years. From the perspective of professional advisors, the act of delivering money management advice has always tended to be a fairly conservative discipline. But for their clients, especially those who have inherited sizeable estates, "conservative" spending of inherited assets is seldom the case.

We are not suggesting that the fundamental mechanics of traditional financial and estate planning have not changed since William and Mary chartered the Bank of England. On the contrary, the increase in the variety and complexity of the tools, products and strategies available to advisors in the past twenty-five years alone is nothing short of breathtaking. Further, the evolution of the World Wide Web, and its implications for the financial world has created more than a paradigm shift: it is *cataclysmic* in its implications for the future, at least from a transactional perspective. Many people feel that the immediacy and totality of information from the net is a major boon to financial planning.

The web certainly delivers in that department. (Scientists at the CERN particle physics laboratory in Switzerland recently sent a full-length DVD movie—*Star Wars*, what else?!—to colleagues at the California Institute of Technology in one half of one second, more than thirty thousand times faster than a typical home broadband connection.) More information faster. Sophisticated analytical tools. Plus, of course, cool, user-friendly interfaces. All designed to complete more transactions at a greater speed and with higher efficiency than ever before in history. We don't just live in an information age, we are awash in information.

This deluge of facts, statistics and news may well be the most significant development in the history of human knowledge, with tremendous implications for each of us. So great is the impact that more and more contemporary scholars are saying that we may be witnessing the end of history as we have known it.

, , ,

Consider:

The University of California, Berkeley, has a *"How Much Information"* project, which studies the amount of information produced each year. In 2008, Americans consumed information for about 1.3 trillion hours, an average of almost 12 hours per day per person. Consumption by all Americans totaled 3.6 zettabytes and 10,845 trillion words, which works out to 100,500 words and

34 gigabytes for an average person on an average day. (A zettabyte is 10 to the 21st power bytes, a million million gigabytes, by the way.) These estimates are from an analysis of more than 20 different sources of information, from very old (newspapers and books) to very new (portable computer games, satellite radio, and Internet video). And while you are still contemplating just how big these numbers are, the statistics we just noted do not include the amount of information consumed at work!

Of course, there is more…

• A single issue of the daily New York Times now contains more information than the seventeenth century man or woman would have encountered in a lifetime.

• A (possibly apocryphal) story tells that, at only twelve years of age, John Stuart Mill had read the entire amount of written information available in the world in English and French. Today, only a hundred and fifty years later, as we go from grade school to high school we learn only *one billionth* of what there is to learn. There is enough scientific information written every day to fill seven complete sets of the *Encyclopedia Britannica*; there is enough scientific information written every year to keep a person busy reading day and night for four hundred sixty years!

• Moore's Law (by Gordon Moore, co-founder of Intel) in computing says that information processing doubles in speed every 18 months.

• The sum total of human knowledge now doubles every two to three years. (Meaning that your personal knowledge must double every two to three years just to remain at your current level of ability, income and success in your chosen or current field of work.) And you might want to increase your vitamins: by the year 2020, it is expected that the sum total of human knowledge will double *every seventy-two days.*

• More than eighty-five percent of the world's technological knowledge has been developed in this century alone.

• Over 2.2 million new book titles were released last year, and the total of all printed knowledge doubles every four years.

• Scientific information doubles every five years and scientific knowledge doubles every ten years.

• In the last thirty years mankind has produced more information than in the previous five thousand years.

• In his book *Brain Longevity*, Dr. Dharma Singh Khalsa says the average American sees sixteen thousand advertisements, logos and labels in a day.

• The average Fortune 1000 worker already is sending and receiving approximately 276 messages and documents each day.
• Technology reduces the amount of time it takes to do any one task yet increases the number of tasks that people are expected to do(i.e., answering your email).

, , ,

As we plan out our financial lives, including planning for the things that we want to leave to our inheritors, a dearth of information about the endless number of plans and programs available to us isn't an issue. Information we have. Traditional programs to minimize taxes and shelter income, we have. Incredibly sophisticated software tools, that can analyze and assess hundreds of possible financial futures for us with the stroke of a key, we have.

What is missing, what has always been missing, is a broader context underlying the financial and estate plans we develop. A context that is based upon historical reality, one that acknowledges and appreciates the role of the unique values, stories, life lessons and experiences that have shaped and guided you and your family for generations.

We want to be clear that within the framework of traditional financial and estate planning are elements that are, and always will be, important. Ultimately, the numbers must be crunched, the assets allocated, the tax liability landscape surveyed.

However, most traditional estate plans are manufactured in a kind of clinical isolation, cut off from the most critical information required for them be truly successful. Accounting, actuarial and legal formulas are typically applied with "one-size-fits-all" certainty. The estate is regarded in this process as a "thing in itself," separate from living beings, just as it was even before the Statute of Wills transformed the world of inheritance when it was first promulgated in sixteenth century England. In truth, your estate is not an empirically evident or physically tangible "thing in itself." Instead, it is an intertwining set of relationships between you, your ancestors, your children, and generations of your children yet unborn.

Those relationships cannot be quantified mathematically. They cannot be folded into a balance sheet. They defy scientific inquiry. And yet, it is precisely those relationships—and the conditions that will either undermine them or nurture them and make them strong enough to survive for generations—that will determine the success or failure of not just your estate plan, but, more importantly, of your family itself.

# CHAPTER THREE

## I, Being of Sound Mind...
*"Your last will and testament is the wrong place to do your parenting"*
The Authors

When the founder of one of America's largest frozen foods companies died in the mid 1990s, a fortune estimated at over $500 million dollars was to be distributed among a small group of heirs that included his second wife, their three children, his brother and a cousin.

He had been meticulous, almost fastidious, in the management of his business affairs. Workers on the plant floor would tell you that he could walk past a flash-freezing conveyor laden with tons of washed peas, and tell you, within a twelve-ounce box or two, exactly how many packages of frozen peas were in that unit.

His daily life was a model of precision and efficiency. Up at 5:00 a.m. for a one-hour swim, followed by breakfast at the club, then a staff meeting at 8:00 a.m. sharp. Every minute of his day at the office was focused and productive.

He required comprehensive production reports daily, and he could account for every pea, kernel of corn and bit of broccoli from the time it left the farm until it was washed, prepped, frozen, packaged and palletized to the loading dock.

The frozen foods magnate managed his personal life in much the same fashion. In fact, the only blip in his seventy-seven-year personal life was his divorce from a first wife when he was thirty-five. Other than that, he and his second wife had raised three children, served in their church, and supported local charities with a quiet dignity that was the envy of all who knew them.

His estate and business succession planning had been no less carefully considered. A team of seasoned CPAs, investment managers and attorneys crafted a state-of-the art plan that took several years to complete. To see all of the contracts, agreements, trust documents and other legal and financial instruments that comprised his plan laid out on one table was an impressive sight. The frozen foods king kept a set of the plans on the credenza in his office. They sat there for several years, three thick binders larger than the New York City phone directory. It gave him peace of mind to glance over at them from time to time. It was a matter of some pride to him that immediately following his death his estate would be settled seamlessly, and with great decorum. Dignity and efficiency. The hallmarks of his business life would be the legacy of his personal life.

(And now, the sound of a whoopee cushion being deployed with great gusto!)

In fact, within hours of his death, attorneys representing just about everybody the frozen foods baron had ever brushed up against in life were in line to file briefs at the county courthouse. Stays. Writs. Pleadings. Injunctions.

Mr. Flash Freeze's three-volume estate plan, with its elaborate mechanisms focused on minimizing taxes, was pronounced dead at about the same time he was. His first wife, whom he had not seen or talked with in over forty years, wanted *something*. The oldest son wanted *everything*. The middle son wanted *more*, the daughter's husband (no doubt deep in grief over the loss of his father-in-law) decided they should hold off on their own divorce proceedings, and instead convinced her she should have a role in managing the company. His cousin's demand for money was based on a claim that he had secretly helped invent the company's first flash-freezing system, while the brother figured he had been out on the loading dock long enough to deserve a spot in the head office.

As for the grieving widow, her instructions to the phalanx of lawyers assembled to join in battle was short and simple: "To hell with them all. None of them deserves a dime."

The family and their legal representatives slugged it out until 2007. Several million dollars were spent on legal and accounting fees. The traditional Christmas gathering at the parents' house has been on hold for more than a decade. And none of the kids is talking to mom—let alone to one another.

The advisors to the frozen-foods baron had constructed a great plan. What no one had done, what few ever do, was to spend an equal amount of time and energy *preparing the heirs* for the receipt of that plan.

Welcome to the real world of estate planning—American style.

, , ,

Over the past century we have developed a sophisticated system of death planning built upon a single overriding premise:

*The goal of estate planning is to preserve accumulated assets from taxes.*

To be sure, we could add that its purpose is also to mitigate attorneys' fees and administrative costs, but the central objective of death planning in America has been, and remains, to preserve the assets accumulated in the present generation for the succeeding generation.

According to Paul Schervish of Boston College, at least forty-one trillion dollars will pass from one generation to the next by the year 2044.[1] It's probably fair to say most of it will be passed from this generation to the next with the same mindset: *protect the accumulated assets.* It's also fair to say that the success rate of those traditional plans (when measured out across two to three generations) will be about the same as the success rate of parents in getting their three-year-olds to eat the mushy *"freezer to microwave"* vegetable medley that our frozen food friend pioneered.

Which begs the question: if the track record for traditional estate planning is so bad, why has it been the dominant planning process?

Imagine a powerful steam locomotive barreling down the track, with a clear sky, a strong tailwind, and an energetic crew feeding the boiler nonstop. An engine that continues to gather momentum as it climbs to the highest mountain pass with only a slight reduction in speed, then gathers more speed and energy as it descends to the valley below. It is unstoppable. There is abundant fuel, and fresh crews stand ready to relieve the boiler stokers whenever they tire. The engineers and crew never look back. Their eyes are fixed only on the distant horizon. There is no end planned for the journey. They just keep going.

This is a quintessentially American attitude. It fueled the growth of the most dynamic economy the world has ever seen. Through boom and bust, war and peace, the energy behind the American locomotive has never faltered.

In "The Greatest Century That Ever Was," Stephen Moore and Julian L. Simon wrote:

"More financial wealth has been generated in the United States over the past fifty years than was created in all the rest of the world in all the centuries before 1950. Fifty years ago, real financial wealth was about five trillion in 1998 dollars. By 1970, that financial wealth had doubled to roughly ten trillion dollars. Since then the value of Americans' financial wealth has tripled to over thirty trillion. When we combine this burst in financial assets with the sevenfold real increase in housing equity owned by Americans, we discover that the nation's assets have risen from about six trillion to more than forty trillion dollars in real terms in the past half century."

America has been, and continues to be, an economic engine of prodigious proportions and astounding output. By any material standard imaginable, the quality of life today far surpasses that of one hundred years ago.

Wages? In 1910, the average hourly pay for a skilled worker (in today's dollars) was $3.43. Less than minimum wage today. By 1950, that hourly rate had increased to $9.70 per hour, and today, the average manufacturing wage in the United States is $34.74 an hour, including benefits like health care, retirement plans, vacations, etc.

Productivity? Agricultural production is five to ten times higher than what it was seventy-five years ago, and real per capita gross domestic product has risen from $4,800 in 1910 to $49,000 in 2012.

We're working fewer hours, too. Your grandfather didn't exaggerate about that; in 1850, the average work-week was sixty-six hours.

## Growth in Material Wealth: A Very Long View

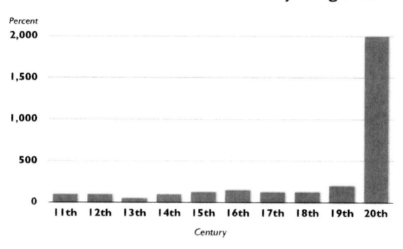

Professor J. Bradford De Long, University of California, *Slouching Towards Utopia*

By 1910, it was fifty hours. Today, the American worker averages just thirty-five hours per week on the job.

Leisure? We have twice as much leisure time as our great-great-grandparents, and, of course, luxuries they couldn't begin to imagine- from flush toilets and indoor showers to air conditioners, microwave ovens, DVD players, and ever more powerful computers.

That's not to say we don't have our share of problems as we enter the twenty-first century. For every benefit there has been an equally significant cost. But, from a purely material standpoint, this much is certain: we have made extraordinary progress in the past century, and that progress has brought incalculable benefit to all of us—regardless of income level. There is simply no comparison between poverty as it exists in America today, and poverty as it was (and still remains in many parts of the world) a hundred years ago.

The above graph shows that the growth in material wealth has been explosive. In the spirit of *"a picture is worth a thousand words,"* it also demonstrates why the message of this book is so important now.

, , ,

So, in answer to the question, the estate planning system in America is the way it is because the system is the natural offspring of a century of amazing economic progress and boundless opportunity. Through the rigorous application of sweat and intellect, thousands of people rose from poverty to amass enormous personal fortunes in the late 1800s and early 1900s. People like Commodore Vanderbilt and John D. Rockefeller, Andrew Carnegie and J.P. Morgan. Leland Stanford, Colis P. Huntington, and Jay Gould.

The world had never seen wealth of this magnitude earned so quickly by so many. It took fewer than thirty years after the end of the Civil War for a uniquely American version of nobility to emerge. Men who could make presidents.

Their pronouncements on political or economic issues could send shivers of fear rippling through the national economy.

When J.P. Morgan decided to establish an umbrella corporation for American steel, he knew he first had to buy out Andrew Carnegie, who owned the most powerful steel company in the world. In 1901, Morgan asked Charles Schwab, the President of Carnegie Steel, to find out whether Carnegie would be willing to sell. Schwab went to see Carnegie on the golf course and presented Morgan's idea. Carnegie replied that he would think about it overnight, and, the next day, he returned with a piece of paper on which he had written in pencil, $480,000,000. That would be the selling price.

Schwab took the piece of paper down to Morgan on Wall Street. Morgan took one look, nodded his head, and said, "I accept this price." It took Morgan only a few weeks to put together a syndicate that purchased other steel companies and railroads and ore lands and steamships and barges. He capitalized U.S. Steel on March 3, 1901, at $1.4 billion. It was the largest corporation in the world.

(When you realize that the entire federal government was spending only about $300 million a year in 1901, and Carnegie's asking price was considerably more than that, you get some appreciation of the size of the fortunes these tycoons held and the kind of power that much wealth represented.)

By 1925, there were more mansions per capita in Rhode Island, New York and Massachusetts than in any of the great cities of Europe. The families of the great bankers and industrialists lived a gilded life of parties, theaters, and world travel.

The New York Times referred to the founders of these fortunes as "colossuses astride the globe." Their sons were "kings-in-waiting."

, , ,

All that money. All that power. And, ultimately, all that misfortune.

Unfortunately, there was no relationship between the ability of the founder to make the fortune, and that of the children to develop a healthy relationship with the money. Andrew Carnegie's religious faith led him to the conclusion that such wealth should be put to use for the betterment of humanity; he subsequently gave most of his money to public libraries and other charities. He had no illusions about the effect of unearned money on children. In a letter to a friend, Carnegie said:

*"The parent who leaves his son enormous wealth generally deaden the talents and energies of the son and tempts him to lead a less useful and less worthy life than he otherwise would."*

, , ,

Cornelius Vanderbilt

That condition describes many of the children of the American tycoons. Cornelius Vanderbilt created one of the greatest fortunes in world history, valued at his death (in 2007 dollars) at $167 billion. He left 95% of his estate to one son, and divided the rest among his eight daughters and his wife, leaving a tiny portion to charity.

Four of his children contested the will, and one ultimately killed himself over the escalating feud about the financial inheritance.

William K. Vanderbilt (1849-1920), grandson of the Commodore, spent his time engaging in leisure sports such as yachting, auto racing, and horse racing. His summer home at Newport, Rhode Island, was modeled after the Petit Trianon at Versailles. It featured five hundred thousand cubic feet of white marble, and custom-made furnishings by J. Allard and Sons of Paris. He employed a summer staff of thirty-six maroon liveried butlers, maids, coachmen, and footmen.

Vanderbilt's lavish lifestyle was extraordinary, at least for its excess. How he felt about the impact his family's wealth had on his own life was another matter. He wrote to a favorite cousin:

*"It has left me with nothing to hope for, with nothing definite to seek or strive for. Inherited wealth is a real handicap to happiness. It is as certain death to ambition as cocaine is to morality."*

Economist John Kenneth Galbraith said that the Vanderbilts showed "both the talent for acquiring money and the dispensing of it in unmatched volume," adding that, "they dispensed their wealth for frequent and unparalleled self-gratification and very often did it with downright stupidity."

Confirmation of that view came only forty-eight years after Cornelius' death: one of his direct descendants died penniless. And, within seventy years of his passing, the last of the ten great Vanderbilt Fifth Avenue mansions in New York City was torn down.

So great was the destruction of the Vanderbilt family and its wealth that for decades through the mid 1900's the press referred to it as "The Fall of the House of Vanderbilt."

Cornelius employed a legion of attorneys and accountants. In fact, his planning was based completely upon the "two-legged stool" of estate and financial planning that dominate the planning arena to this day. He did not consciously prepare his children to receive their inheritances, create a pattern of communication amongst the family, or organize them for ongoing success. Simply stated, he did not prepare his heirs for their inheritance before dropping one of the world's great fortunes into their laps.

The result: when the Vanderbilt family held a reunion in 1973, there were no millionaires left among them.

, , ,

The Vanderbilt story could have turned out far differently. Consider the story of the Rothschild family, which shows how a family can intentionally prepare and organize its children to be strong, independent and successful on their own, apart from the family and its vast fortune.

The family first rose to prominence in the late 18th century under Mayer Amschel Rothschild, and, by the time Sir Nathan Rothschild came to lead the family's enterprises at the turn of the 20th century, the name Rothschild was synonymous with banking and finance. So great was their power that on several occasions the House of Rothschild, as it came to be known, actually bailed Germany and England out of economic catastrophes that could have lead to their collapse.

The Rothschild family philosophy on passing inheritances from one generation to the next is very different from Vanderbilt's, whom we discussed earlier. The family motto for over two centuries has been "Strength through Unity."

The Rothschilds actively mentor the children, from one generation to the next. For example, they establish family banks to lend money to those children who wish to start businesses or pursue other careers, and they monitor and advise the ventures in which the children participate.

At the annual family gatherings (which have been held for over 200 years), the values which have sustained the family for generations are affirmed even as their vision for the future is sharpened and clarified. (And, if a family member fails to attend the annual family gathering, they are locked out of the family bank!) As part of that vision, the extended family, from Europe to the United States, supports a lively program of philanthropy in the arts, medicine, science and education.

Commodore Vanderbilt focused on Financial Planning, which grows and protects the money, and Estate Planning, which prepares the money for the heirs. The Rothschilds added a third "leg": they use their own variation of heritage design, which prepares the heirs to receive their inheritance. Building on that very stable platform has been the key to keeping individual family members—and the family as a whole—unified, strong and prosperous for generations, no matter what is happening in the world around them.

> *"It requires a great deal of boldness and a great deal of caution to make a great fortune; and when you have got it, it requires 10 times more wit to keep it."* Nathan Rothschild

⸙ ⸙ ⸙

The phenomenal burst of economic activity in the late 1800s produced huge personal fortunes, and the sheer dimensions of this newly-minted wealth created a demand for specialized managers to shepherd and protect it. The rise of the great tycoons and the evolution of a thriving middle class of professionals with disposable income in the late nineteenth and early twentieth centuries gave birth to a new class of professional money managers, personal bankers, investment strategists and attorneys. Their job: to grow their clients' personal assets and to protect them from the icy grasp of stockholders, competitors, and the government. With scant exception, it is exactly what financial and legal advisors to the affluent do today.

The accountants and attorneys of the early 1900s were not charged with, or concerned about, the behavior of their clients' children. Their labors were undertaken with pen and ink, computation pads and legal briefs. (Family counseling did not exist. And families kept their secrets in their closets.)

Their legal and fiduciary responsibilities were considerable—and so was the compensation. Some of the great investment and banking houses in America today were founded by the very accountants who once served the tycoons, who soon accumulated vast family fortunes of their own.

With the passing years, the tools professional money managers could employ on behalf of their clients grew in complexity. They also increased the emotional/personal distance between advisor and client. You can't do business on a handshake anymore.

By the early 1930s, the accounting and investment management fields had developed elaborate, highly technical sets of operational procedures and rules to govern their professions and to set standards for their work product. In conjunction with the regulations of the new Securities and Exchange Commission and other regulatory boards and agencies, a bold new world of money management and financial and estate planning emerged. A highly regulated, formalized, quantifiable world.

In large part because of various security scandals, the effects of the Depression, and the increasing government regulation and oversight which resulted, the job of advisor to the affluent became an increasingly defensive profession. The take-charge, innovative, take-the-offensive kind of money management that characterized the period from the Civil War up until the 1920s was gone forever— even if modern advertising would have you believe the opposite. Financial and estate planners were now operating from a different perspective. Their jobs were to protect and defend.

Defend the asset base against all comers. Protect profits from the government. Defend against potential lawsuits, unnecessary regulation, even against unwelcome and undeserving would-be inheritors. Defend against everything except the collapse and destruction of the family they served.

, , ,

Traditional estate planning hasn't changed much since the Roaring Twenties. Tax policies come and go, and new financial products pop up in response to changing legal and economic circumstances. Through it all, advisors to the affluent have pretty much maintained a respectable arms length distance from the client's personal life and values base. Their task then, as now, was to manage and defend wealth; and, until very recently, the health of the client's family itself was not a part of the "wealth" equation.

That is changing. In fact, the areas of responsibility within which the estate planning advisor works is undergoing a major overhaul right now, starting with the rejection of the old idea that the client can be defined by the list of assets he or she owns.

As crazy as it sounds, advisors have never worked from the assumption that a family, like any organization, is more than the sum total of its parts. Many advisors look at the client's family from a mathematical, static viewpoint. That is, if (a) the purpose of estate planning is to protect accumulated assets, then (b) the distribution of those assets through the payout line known as the inheritors should be planned for with the same sterile objectivity as the plans made for reducing or eliminating federal and state taxes.

So, the net objective of most traditional planning has been to generate plans that will get as many goodies as possible out of the deceased's estate, past the IRS, and into the anxious embrace of waiting family members. Under this simple system, success is measured at the time the checks are made out to the inheritors. What happens the next day? Well… that just hasn't been the advisor's concern.

Anyway, the men and women who built the engine that is the American economy weren't in the habit of looking back—let alone to the side. What worked for their businesses would work for their families. As long as the locomotive boiler was stoked with fuel (money), their families would prosper and continue to move ahead.

But, we know that 9 out of 10 inheritances ultimately fail. Why is that? And how is it that with all that money and power behind them those family locomotives run out of fuel and get pushed off the track?

To understand why inheritances fail, it is a good idea to begin with the money itself. Lots and lots of it...

# CHAPTER FOUR

## Sudden Wealth

*"How long does the average recipient of an inheritance wait before they buy a new car? Just nineteen days."* New Car Dealer Association

On a clear autumn morning in 1949, Jack Wrum stirred from his sleep under a park bench in Sausalito, California, just north of San Francisco. He bummed change for a cup of coffee, then headed down to Dunphy Park to see what the tides in Richardson Bay had washed up onto the beach the night before.

As he filled his burlap bag with tin, glass and bits of anything he might be able to sell, Wrum spotted what appeared to be a green wine bottle poking out of a mound of brown seaweed. To his surprise, the bottle was corked—and the cork was sealed under a thick layer of some kind of wax. Things were looking up! He usually preferred his wine before his coffee, but, on a day as beautiful as this, he was prepared to bend the rules of etiquette.

Plopping down beside the pile of seaweed, he began to saw away at the wax and cork with his pocketknife. In a moment the old bottle was open. To his great disappointment, there was no wine inside. Instead, he found a piece of paper, rolled tight with a rubber band.

Wrum unrolled the note and read:

*To avoid confusion, I leave my entire estate to the lucky person who finds this bottle, and to my attorney, Barry Cohen, share and share alike.*

*Daisy Alexander, June 20, 1937.*

Wrum may have been a homeless beachcomber, but he knew opportunity when he saw it. He pocketed the note and went in search of the first attorney he could find. Within weeks, the story unfurled. Daisy Alexander was Daisy *Singer* Alexander, heiress to the Singer Sewing Machine company fortune. When Daisy died, she left twelve million dollars, company stock, and a letter to her British solicitor instructing that her legal will would "turn up in good time."

And turn up it did. One evening several years before her death, Daisy walked from her London home to the center of a footbridge above the Thames River. She drew the sealed wine bottle from her coat and tossed it into the dark water. The bottle drifted down the Thames and was carried by currents up into the North Sea. The Barents Sea pushed it across the northern coasts of Scandinavia, along the rocky shores of Russia and Siberia, then down into the Bering Straits and into the Pacific Ocean, where it drifted south until finally, after nearly twelve years, it washed ashore in a clump of seaweed near San Francisco.

An expert in ocean currents testified that it would take about twelve years for a bottle to travel from London to San Francisco. The bottle was found eleven years and eight months after the date on the will. Daisy Singer's will was authenticated. Jack Wrum received six million dollars, plus ongoing income from his share of Singer stock. Not a bad day's beachcombing.

, , ,

History doesn't record what became of beachcomber Jack and his remarkable windfall, and that's probably just as well. The one recurring problem among people who have inherited money out of the blue is that most of them end up struggling to come to grips with the effects of sudden wealth.

That's because who we were the day before the inheritance was received, or the lottery winnings paid out, is who we are the day after.

We have the same strengths, the same flaws, the same habits. Character is not improved by the sudden receipt of money. It is revealed by it. (That explains the new car in nineteen days. And, while you might have guessed as much, when we ask parents "What's the last thing you want your children to do when they get their inheritance, the overwhelming answer is: "We don't want them to go out and buy a new car!") If we didn't have a healthy relationship with money before we became rich, that relationship will only grow more problematic as we suddenly find ourselves awash in money, with ramifications that can ultimately destroy the things we love the most.

To appreciate the potential danger and power that the sudden inheritance of money can have on a person, it's important to note that there are different kinds of inheritances that we can give or receive. Most of us think of things like property, stocks, bonds, or cash when we think of what constitutes an inheritance. Of course, lots of inheritance problems could be nipped in the bud if the inheritors simply understood that most estates consist of real estate and securities, not cash. Those securities are often closely held, part of the family business. So, the siblings they are about to go to war with over the estate assets just might end up being partners in business.

And here is an important note: the dangers inherent in receiving sudden wealth are not restricted to those who received huge fortunes in the millions of dollars. When Rod Zeeb asks audiences made up of people with average incomes "how much inherited money do you think it takes to hurt a child or grandchild," he has never had a group come up with an answer higher than $100,000. Rod then asks, "so, how many of *you* are going to leave your children or grandchildren $100,000 or more?"

It doesn't take all that much money to destroy a life.

, , ,

For hundreds of years, estate planning has focused on these *financial* inheritances almost exclusively. But there is another kind of inheritance that we receive and give, an inheritance that is far more powerful, and ultimately more meaningful, than money.

That is an *emotional* inheritance: one that we receive over a lifetime from other family members, friends, teachers, religious leaders, coaches and other significant people in our lives.

There is a great difference between the financial inheritance we *may* receive from our parents or grandparents and the emotional inheritance we *will* receive from them no matter the size of their material estates. Metaphorically speaking, they are apples and oranges.

Financial inheritances are easy to understand: they are material and quantifiable. Traditional estate planning has any number of strategies to protect the assets from taxation in order to deliver the maximum amount to the heirs. In traditional estate planning, money is the exclusive focus, the guiding star, and the only real concern of the legal process. It is the beginning—and for most, the ending—of the estate planning cycle. Of course, since we know that most traditional estate plans begin to crumble almost as quickly as they begin to shower assets upon the heirs, one might be tempted to call money the "time bomb" inheritance.

Emotional inheritances bear no relationship whatsoever to financial inheritances. They are composed not of things, but of the values, stories, life lessons and experiences that you lived with and absorbed (to one degree or another) from your parents, grandparents, and other important people in your life. These people of influence may have taught you these things explicitly, or you may have picked them up simply through the act of living and interacting with and around them. It is this emotional inheritance (added to and enriched by your own life experience and living example) that you will pass on to your family and other people you know, whether or not you leave anything that might be described as a financial inheritance. The emotional legacy is no less than the sum total of your life experience as evidenced by the way you lived.

You received an emotional inheritance from your parents or grandparents while they lived. Your own children or grandchildren are receiving theirs from you right now. The discovery, articulation and incorporation of the core components that constitute your emotional inheritance into the framework of your estate planning is what heritage design (and *The Heritage Process*™) are all about.

In effect, heritage design redefines the traditional concept of wealth to include not only money and other financial assets, but also the values, history and lessons that make life meaningful, fulfilling and ultimately successful, from one generation to the next.

Heritage design acknowledges the importance of the financial assets, but mostly in respect to their primary function as a resource and tool to help perpetuate the things that really matter, the things that hundreds of years of experience and research have shown are the only way to keep your family strong and prosperous for generations.

, , ,

There are reasons why 9 out of 10 inheritances fail. In short, even the best, most artfully constructed plan cannot compensate for an unprepared heir. When money is the primary focus of estate planning, inheritors often equate their self-worth with their net worth. Jessie O'Neill, author of *The Golden Ghetto: The Psychology of Affluence* (herself an heir in a wealthy family), describes the impact that a financial inheritance can have on people who receive a financial inheritance without an emotional inheritance—that is, money without meaning. She lists the following outcomes of the condition known as "affluenza," defined as a dysfunctional relationship with money, or the improper pursuit of it:

- Inability to delay gratification • Inability to tolerate frustration • Low future motivation • Low self-esteem • Low self-worth • Lack of self-confidence • Lack of personal identity • Social and emotional isolation • Feelings of depression, failure, anxiety • Unrealistic expectations and lack of accountability • False sense of entitlement •Inability to form intimate relationships

People who receive sudden money without any accompanying values often become hoarders. Or, conversely, they may become habitual over spenders, shopping with no concern for their dwindling bank balances. Quite often, they use money as a tool to control others, particularly family members. Controllers can devastate their children's lives, dangling money like a carrot on a stick to "encourage" children to go to the right school, get the right job, or marry the right person. Many inheritors also use money to gain approval of others, including their own children. They may join exclusive country clubs, or buy a much-too-expensive home in an exclusive neighborhood.

, , ,

We know a man who was the proverbial skinny, pimply-faced nerd at his high school. He went on to make a fortune developing shopping malls along the California coast. So painful were his memories of being picked on and abused in high school that he decided to try to re-invent himself in the minds of all those who had ignored him for those four long years. For his twenty-fifth high school reunion he chartered a 747 to fly three hundred members of his graduating class to Italy, where they cruised the Adriatic Sea for ten days on a luxury liner. Despite his largesse, however, none of his classmates have continued any kind of friendship or relationship with him since the cruise.

The symptoms and manifestations of this dysfunctional relationship with wealth make up a pretty depressing litany of disorders. The whole idea of affluenza flies in the face of what most people believe their lives would be like if one day, just like Jack Wrum, they came upon the proverbial pot of gold. "If I only had money," the fantasy begins. "People would like me. I would be respected. I would be free to do whatever I wished, whenever I wished to do it. I could take charge of my life, and I would have a sense of absolute security. Nothing could intimidate me, and I would have power. Real power. Most importantly, I would be happy."

It's a great fantasy. An enormously seductive fantasy.

Imagine waking up tomorrow to discover that you have inherited one hundred million dollars from a long-lost uncle. You can immediately satisfy your every desire. You have the wherewithal to buy any home, any consumer toy, piece of art, luxury automobile, even companionship. Jet to Fiji tomorrow? Why not? Spring in the Hamptons? Dinner at Maxim's? Why not, why not, and why not again. Life is meant to be lived. Fully. That's the essence of the financial fantasy, after all. If the opportunity to indulge every fantasy, every whim, every physical or emotional desire should drop in your lap, what are you going to do? Brush it away like a hot coal that popped out of the fire?

(For starters, you might want to try to forget the Yiddish proverb that says *"If you want to know how God feels about money, look who He chooses to make rich."* )

Let's face it; the only thing the world celebrates more than money are the people who have it. In any survey of *America's most admired people,* high profile media, sports and business celebrities always rank high. But, other than wealth, for what are these people really known?

Are they famous for their philanthropy? For their vocal support of education? Their vigorous stance against drug abuse? Their understanding and compassion for people from all walks of life? For being the kind of friends, husbands, wives, daughters upon whom you can really count?

They are famous because they are rich, period. Not one survey respondent in ten thousand could tell you in what these media darlings really believe, what they stand for, or what they have done for the betterment of the world they share with the "little people." It's certainly possible that their families could answer those questions. They may in fact be generous to a fault with charities and other worthy causes. As free-market supporters ourselves, the fact that they are wealthy is just fine with us.

It is the larger point we wish to make: the point that people's perception of the affluent is colored more by the idea that money equals virtue, than by the reality of what the affluent person did to get that money, or for what they actually use it.

For many people, the possession of gobs of money is the greatest, noblest achievement to which one can aspire. In such a culture, should we be surprised if heirs get their priorities out of kilter?

, , ,

The trendy shops along Rodeo Drive in Beverly Hills sell the rarest and most expensive baubles imaginable. South Beach plastic surgeons can turn a toad into a prince (or at least a shiny-faced likeness of one). But boutiques don't sell character, and plastic surgery can't remove our hidden insecurities with the touch of a scalpel. We are, each of us, the product of a lifetime of experience that no amount of cash falling on our heads from heaven can alter. The sudden receipt of *"money without meaning"* only magnifies the personal weaknesses with which each of us lives, no matter our station in life.

There is no denying that money bestows great power upon those who possess it. But there is a limit to what money can actually provide. Money will buy a luxurious bed, but it cannot guarantee a good night's sleep. It can buy a magnificent library, but not brains, nor the discipline to educate yourself; gourmet food but not a healthy appetite. Money can buy designer clothing and jewelry, but not true beauty. It can purchase a house, but never a home; state-of-the-art medicine but not health; luxuries but not culture or taste; temporary amusements but not lasting happiness; religion but not salvation. Money, in fact, can buy a ticket to just about everywhere but heaven.

People who receive sudden wealth like to tell themselves and their friends that their new found treasure hasn't changed their perception of themselves. And that may be true. But money certainly changes the way others will perceive you. An ancient Chinese proverb says: If you are poor, though you dwell in the busy marketplace, no one will inquire about you; if you are rich, though you dwell in the heart of the mountains, you will have distant relatives.

, , ,

What does affluenza look like in real life? Meet a real client, named William. He comes from a middle-class family in Portland, Oregon. His father was a pipe fitter; his mom took in sewing and laundry. William excelled in high school, but his family couldn't afford college, and his scholarship only paid part of his tuition. So William worked his way through school. During the school term, he worked as a waiter, a short-order cook, and a plumber's assistant. Each summer he worked as a deckhand on an Alaskan fishing boat. He even picked fruit and vegetables in Oregon's fertile Willamette Valley farms to pay his way.

His work ethic, his enthusiasm and his drive were just amazing.

No one was surprised when William graduated at the top of his class. He went to work for a machine parts manufacturer and took on every job they had, from maintenance to machine operations, outside sales to personnel management. Eight years later, he started his own manufacturing business in a small rented warehouse. By age fifty-nine he had a net worth in excess of $10 million dollars.

Like many people who become successful through hard work and great personal sacrifice, William made a vow: his kids would never have to work as hard as he did. They wouldn't have to give up parties and football games, and they wouldn't have to buy clothes at Goodwill. They would have everything he didn't—and more. They spent summers at expensive camps and had credit cards by age fourteen. At sixteen they were given keys to their own cars. When it came time for college William made sure they would be able to concentrate on studies and social activities; none ever had so much as a part-time summer job.

In short, William made sure they grew up without a single one of the experiences that had shaped his own life. So, how have the children done?

It has been a bumpy road. William's three children, ranging in age from twenty-three to thirty, have two failed marriages, one bankrupt start-up business, and several drug and alcohol rehab visits between them. Two did graduate from college, but only one currently works at a full-time job. William has tried to bring them into his business, but they just aren't interested. He is so distressed by his children's lack of ambition and motivation that he has decided to sell his business rather than leave any part of it to them.

William's situation is more the rule than the exception among first generation wealth builders. When his story (with names changed to protect everybody) is told at estate planning seminars, planners, attorneys, non-profit officers and others nod their heads in understanding all over the auditorium. They have all seen "Williams" in their practices. Nevertheless, like most traditional financial and legal professionals, their focus is on minimizing risk and growing wealth, not on helping client families identify values that can be used as a foundation for estate planning.

We've all heard about—or seen firsthand—the effects of sudden wealth on people, even if only on a small scale. We read about the tire store worker who wins millions in the lottery and is broke two years later. Or the teenager who gets a small inheritance from a grandparent and blows it on clothing and parties in a matter of days. As for movie stars and rock divas, well, the less said about their excesses, the better.

Still, this is all anecdotal evidence. Is there really that strong a case for a cause and effect relationship between the receipt of sudden wealth and the onset of affluenza? Can't people like William's children—despite having no special training in money management or much life or work experience in the "real world"—learn to successfully manage wealth and keep their families intact on their own and avoid the Midas Curse?

Rod often tells the "Williams" of the world a story he adapted from *The Power of Failure* by Charles Manz. It illustrates a basic truth about the root causes of affluenza.

, , ,

A man sat on his deck, watching a Monarch butterfly struggle to break free of its cocoon. The butterfly twisted and turned, pushing its tiny body against the resilient walls of the cocoon. Its small mouth gnawed a tiny opening at one end, which it slowly and persistently worked to enlarge. Time and again, the butterfly pushed and poked and gnawed, only to fall quiet, exhausted from its efforts. Then, another push, another twist, then collapse. Over and over, the butterfly fought to be free of its cocoon.

After an hour of relentless struggle, the butterfly seemed to give up. It lay still for several minutes, with the tip of its head barely emerging from the elastic cocoon. The man decided that unless he intervened, the butterfly would die. He went inside his house and got a pair of scissors. He made a few delicate cuts along the length of the cocoon, and peeled it back from the body of the butterfly.

The butterfly quickly stirred and immediately unfurled its wings. But the man saw that the body of the butterfly was swollen and lumpy, the wings were shriveled and small. Even the characteristic brilliant orange and black hues of the Monarch were faded.

The misshapen butterfly crawled around the deck for a few minutes, and then died.

The man wanted to understand why the butterfly died, so he called a professor of entomology at the local university. The professor told him that in his attempt to ease the butterfly's struggle he had actually caused its death. For a butterfly to build the strength and stamina to live, the professor said, it had to fight hard to emerge from the cocoon. And the process of slowly squeezing out of the tight cocoon walls actually forces fluid from the butterfly's body and into its wings, enabling it to fly.

The man's intentions were understandable, said the professor. It is difficult to watch any creature struggle. And yet, it is only from the struggle that the butterfly achieves the essential characteristics and abilities it needs to live.

, , ,

It is the same with people. What was the cliché we always heard as kids when we were forced to complete an unpleasant task? "It builds character." Clichés become clichés because they are generally true. Our character *is* shaped by the way we face the struggles in our lives. Especially in the way we deal with failure. The authors of this book have sat with hundreds of self-made affluent people, some with net worths in the billions of dollars. When they ask about the paths these people carved out on their road to financial success, there is one theme they hear over and over. To become successful, they are told, you need to learn to *fail well*. Learn to fail in a way that prepares you for greater success. Understand that learning and personal growth, skill development, courage, persistence, the potential for empathy and other important life assets, all come from your struggles, and especially from your failures.

If we seek to avoid challenges, if we shy away from setbacks, if we hide from the world or give up on our dreams when we fail, we will never learn the skills and abilities necessary to thrive and prosper, in both our business and personal lives. Experiencing failure gives us the opportunity to wrestle with the kind of challenges that squeeze life-giving fluid into our own wings and prepare us for successful flight in life.

It is important to note that William's problem is not that he does not love his kids. Clearly, he wants the best for them. He just never realized that the very values and ethics that brought him success—like hard work, sacrifice, and goal-setting—are the most valuable assets he possesses. How—or whether—he transmits them to his children is the single most important determinant of how successful they, and later their children, will be in building strong families of their own and in managing and growing the material assets they will be given.

For estate planning to succeed across generations, and for families to remain strong, the emotional inheritance must be identified and communicated to the inheritors. (John L. Levy, a psychological consultant who specializes in the problems of inheritors, says that most of the problems in inheritance could be prevented if people simply *talked* with their parents about these issues before they die!)

That emotional inheritance becomes the framework for planning that puts *family* before *fortune* by focusing on the things of value, rather than on the value of things. As a result, the money remains a tool—not a cure, not a fix, not the answer to a prayer—and not the focus of the estate plan. And the purpose of that tool is simple: to support a family vision that reflects, honors and supports the values that helped earn the wealth in the first place.

Remember that forty-one trillion dollars that will pass from one generation to the next over the next three decades? That transfer—the largest asset shift in the history of the planet—can enhance the lives of families, strengthen their relationships, support the causes in which they believe and benefit countless philanthropic organizations.

Or, it could really make the day of those boutique owners along Rodeo Drive.

# CHAPTER FIVE

## What Will Get *You?*

*"If we would have new knowledge, we must get a whole new world of questions."* Susanne K. Langer

Imagine that you are the great-grandchild of a hardworking entrepreneur who built a company worth tens of millions of dollars—from the ground up. Now, apply the historical 90% failure rate odds to your mythical family situation. Assume that your grandparents and great aunts and uncles burned through 70% of the fortune your grandfather worked so hard to accumulate, and then your parents and their siblings ate through most of the rest. (Don't be too angry. Remember, this inexorable soap opera of loss and family chaos has been the norm since ancient times.)

One evening as you sit outside your manufactured home enjoying a hearty can of chili, a professor from the local college arrives for an appointment. He is doing research on the causes of multi-generational wealth loss, and he has been told that you have intimate knowledge of exactly how it is that one generation earns it, the next spends it, and the generations that come after are reduced to telling stories about how good the family once had it.

The professor really only has one question: *what got your family?* A simple enough query. And for all of us who (just looking of course) occasionally browse the headlines of the tabloid newspapers in the supermarket checkout lines, a question with some pretty obvious answers. Drugs got 'em. Greed got 'em. Laziness. Bad investments. Bad advice. Bad marriages. Bad luck.

Common sense answers, sure enough, and each with more than a grain of truth in them. Of course, reliance on gut instinct is not always the best way to achieve clarity about issues of great importance. Before we share the results of the actual study that asked that exact question of thousands of people whose families really *did* blow it all, though, let us ask you for your thoughts. For the sake of this exercise, assume that you have built a comfortable estate. Doesn't have to be in the mega-millions, but enough so that you would leave a sizable wad of cash if you died tomorrow. If that were the case (and keeping in mind the 90% probability that, one way or another, the money will be squandered):

"*What do you think will get your family?*"

Take a minute to think about it. Try to jot down at least 4 or 5 things that you think could apply in your unique family situation.

, , ,

In 2009, Family Office Exchange, an association of professionals whose independent offices manage the assets of some of the world's wealthiest families, asked that very question of their clients: *what do you think will get your family*. Don't be surprised if their answers mirror yours.

78% of the respondents in this survey indicated that if their family was to lose it all, the most likely reason would be some combination of poor investments and/or a weak economy.

15% cited miscellaneous causes like drugs, divorce and bad luck as the top probable causes.

7% indicated that the cause would most likely be some aspect of family dynamics.

Those answers certainly make sense, and one would be hard-pressed to find fault with them. But for noted researchers Roy Williams and Vic Preisser, the assumptions within those common sense answers just weren't enough. Like the professor in our example above, they wanted to get the answer from those who actually had experienced the Midas Curse in their own families.

Williams and Preisser's research extended over a period of twenty years and to conversations with over 2,000 families, each of whom actually experienced both a loss of family wealth and family unity. The responses from these families were clear and unequivocal. And, for those of us who were just fine with the tabloid news version of the root causes of the Midas Curse, they also turned the apple cart of assumptions upside down.

Your family had money and lost it, said Williams and Preisser? So, what really happened? Bad investments and under-performing markets? Drugs and divorce? Lousy advice from professionals?

Not exactly, it seems.

60% of the respondents in this extensive study replied that their families lost their assets and were torn apart primarily because of a lack of **communication** and **trust** within the family.

25% said that their family woes were caused because the **heirs were unprepared** for the responsibilities (both financial and emotional) that accompanied their inheritances.

12% cited multiple other causes.

**Just 3%** cited failures in financial planning, investments, taxes and other purely financial causes.

, , ,

As it did with us, the empirical results from this groundbreaking study might set you back on your heels. Heck, there isn't a single supermarket tabloid headline to be found in the conclusions of the Williams and Preisser study. Collective wisdom collides with scientific study. One of them has to give, and in this case, the cultural shibboleth that posits that money and the management thereof is, in and of itself, a root cause of the Midas Curse no longer meets the criteria for an acceptable proof.

In short, the following maxim should be line 1, sentence 1 at the top of every financial planning and estate planning web page and brochure produced from this day forth:

> *"Planning for the future of your money is not the same as planning for the future of your family."*
>
> Rod Zeeb

And if your professional advisor does not get it, you should give serious thought to shopping around for an advisor who does.

## Video Break

We love to read. But, we also appreciate that some people prefer the more kinetic visual and audio learning style provided by video. Where a given concept might fall flat in print for these folks, through video the same concept can spring to life. No doubt the tech community will soon come up with printed books that can also display video on thin paper pages inside a paper cover (Not all of us are ready to turn in our physical books for tablet devices.)

That technology isn't here yet, but, for our readers who really do appreciate and benefit from the video perspective, we have sprinkled this book with a series of "video" vignettes that illustrate fundamental principles of heritage design using a screenplay format

Popcorn is optional.

**VIDEO: Two Funerals**
*Location: Interior / Home Living Room / Day*

This vignette presents two separate "visions"
of the same person's funeral.

We FADE IN as about two-dozen people are
gathered in the living room of Grandmother Pine
following the funeral of her husband, Arthur.
There is food laid out on a sideboard; people
hold plates and glasses as they talk.

**Vision 1:**
We join in on several of the conversations
that are taking place. First, we follow a child
of about six or seven as she makes her way
through the crowded room to where Grandmother
Pine is seated on a couch.
The little girl takes Grandmother's hand,
and says: "Grammy, I'm really going to miss
grandpa."
The grandmother smiles, and asks, "What will
you miss most about him?"
The child replies, "His advice on bond market
fluctuations were spot on, and when he steered
me away from derivatives last year and put me
into T-Bills, I saved a bundle."
"And what's your plan to replace him?' asks
grandmother.
"We'll be interviewing a couple of new
advisors next week, so I don't think losing
granddad will really have any negative impact
on my portfolio," says the girl causally.
Grandmother nods and adds, "Arthur knew
markets and money management. That's what
attracted me to him fifty years ago, and that's

71

what held our marriage together all these years. Why don't I tell you about the way he steered us through the great recession of '83."

As the child and her grandmother settle down on the couch, we join another conversation, this one between Arthur's 40ish son and several other people.

"Dad had the gift, that's for sure," the son is saying as we join the conversation. "And he never wasted a minute of his day on anything frivolous. He would walk in the door at 8 sharp every night after work, have a bite of dinner, and then sit in his chair over there and review the financial section of the newspaper. He would highlight articles he wanted me to clip out and paste into notebooks. They're over there in the bookcase."

The son points out the long line of thick old notebooks with dates on the spines to his admiring friends.

"Do you ever just sit down with one of those notebooks and think back on those times?" asks a friend.

The son laughs. "I suppose I should, but then I wouldn't have time to carry on the tradition with my own son!"

We join another conversation, this one between three women.

The oldest woman in the group says, "Mr. Pine was a good boss. 25 years I worked for him. He never missed a day. Not for birthdays or ball games or holidays, not when his children were sick, never."

"And he never retired?" asked one of the women.

"And miss a market opening?" replied the first woman.

"'Business is who we are and what we do,' he used to say. 'If it's good for the business, it's good for me and for you and for everybody we're connected to.'" The three women nod in assent as we cut to:

A deliveryman comes through the front door with an urgent package. Arthur's son signs for the package, opens it, and then stands on a chair and calls for quiet. As the room stills he says, "Great news everyone. The deal dad was finalizing at the hospital the day he died has been accepted by the Megatron board. The merger is on!"

The room erupts in applause. The little girl hugs Grandmother on the couch, someone hands the deliveryman a glass of champagne. Camera pans through the crowd to the wall behind the couch where we see a framed, old-fashioned hand-embroidered sampler that says: *"What's GOOD for the business is GOOD for the family."*

**Vision Two**

As the chatter and tinkle of glasses fades, we slowly dissolve to the second 'vision' of Arthur's funeral.

We FADE IN to the same scene, same cast of characters, with one addition: a Pastor is also there.

Once again, we follow the little girl as she makes her way through the crowded room to Grandmother Pine's side. The little girl takes Grandmother's hand, and says:

"Grammy, I'm really going to miss grandpa."

The grandmother smiles, and asks, "What will you miss most about him?"

This time, the child replies, "He always asked me what kind of books and games I liked, and he told me lots of funny stories. I remember when I had the measles he brought me a teddy bear that he had painted measles on so I wouldn't feel like I was alone. And once instead of mommy picking me up from school it was Granddad, and we got ice cream and walked through the park and Granddad showed me where he carved his name and yours inside a heart on a tree when he was a teenager. That was my favorite day ever."

Grandmother smiles. "And you will remember that day forever and ever," she says. Grandmothers' eyes brim with tears as she says, "We had a lot of adventures in 50 years of marriage, and we went through our share of difficult times.

"But no matter how tough things got, your grandfather always had time for other people, he treated everyone he came into contact with kindness and respect, and he looked for the good inside people."

"Will you always remember the day granddad carved your name in the tree?" asked the child. Grandmothers eyes brighten, and she gives her granddaughter a hug. "Let's get some punch and I'll tell you all about that day," she says.

As the child and her grandmother get up to fill their glasses, we join another conversation, this one between Arthur's 40ish son and several other people.

"Dad had the gift, that's for sure," the son says as we join the conversation. "He had a way of making you feel ten feet tall no matter how bad you were feeling about something. See those scrapbooks over there?" He points to the bookcase, where the same thick notebooks are lined up.

The son continues, "The truth is I was never a first-string athlete-heck I was barely third string. But that never mattered to my dad; he was there for every ball game, every track meet…whatever sport I was struggling at, he was there. He used to wear a ratty old felt hat, and he'd wave that thing like crazy from the stands to make sure I knew he was up there watching me." The son's voice catches: "But he didn't need to wave, and I didn't need to search him out in the crowd. I always knew he'd be there for me. Just knowing he was there helped me play my best, and even though my best wasn't exactly varsity level, it didn't bother me."

"So, what about the scrapbooks?" asks a friend.

"Not many of my games were mentioned in the local paper," says the son. "And I don't think my name ever made it in any of the few articles that did appear.

That didn't matter to dad. He took pictures at every game, and when we'd get home he would haul out the typewriter and write up his own sports-report. They're not very long, usually just a paragraph or two, what the weather was like, what position I played, stuff like that. From first grade through high school."

His friends look over at the bookcase. "That's quite a legacy," says one friend.

The son nods. "Those scrapbooks are the most

important inheritance my dad is leaving to me."

We join another conversation, this one between the three women we met earlier.

The first woman says, "Mr. Pine was more than a good boss.

He was one of the most decent people I ever met." She chuckles. "And that little business of his? My goodness, I sometimes wonder how he was able to keep it together over the years. He was always dashing out the door to go to his son's games, or to help at some charity function or another. And if we had a birthday in the office? We'd practically shut down after lunch for cake and just for everybody to visit and catch up on one another's lives."

"Remember when Teresa's daughter went missing, and he shut the office down so all of us could go out and help in the search?" says another of the women. "And when they found her safe and sound and he insisted on taking everybody out to celebrate? Seems like he was always celebrating something in somebody's life."

The third woman adds: "Our company could have grown a lot more, Mr. Pine could have made a lot more money. He could have been a millionaire."

The first woman raises her punch glass. "To the richest man I ever knew," she says. The other two women join her in the toast.

We hear a spoon tapping against a glass. It is the Pastor, calling for everyone's attention.

The group quiets, and the Pastor says, "As I listen to the conversations in this room today, I know how pleased Arthur would be that you are all here celebrating your special memories of him. I see a lot of smiles, and I hear a lot of laughter. He would like that. Arthur Pine's true legacy lives on through each of us. That is a remarkable gift…"

As the Pastor continues to talk, the camera pulls back, until his voice can no longer be heard. The camera pans the expression on the faces of the people in the room. We see smiles and soft tears, wistful remembrance and quiet reflection.

Finally, the camera pans through crowd to the wall behind couch where we see a framed, old-fashioned hand-embroidered sampler.

It simply says: *"What's Good for the family is Good for everything else."*

-end-

# CHAPTER SIX

## Introducing Heritage Design: The 3ʳᵈ Element of Successful Multi-Generational Planning

*"The most important question we asked wasn't, why do 90% of families fail. It was, what do the successful 10% of families do differently?"*

The authors

For centuries, the process by which most families have planned for their futures has consisted of two traditional planning elements: financial planning and estate planning. And, as we have noted, for centuries, 9 out of 10 of those plans have ultimately failed the families they were supposed to protect. In about 70% of families, both the assets and the family unity are demolished by the end of the second generation. By the end of the third generation, 90% of families have seen their unity and their assets disappear.

The difference between the 90% of families who fail and the 10% who successfully keep their family unity and their assets together for multiple generations is not in the quality or thoroughness of the financial or estate planning that they do. Most professionals deliver good planning to their clients. The difference is that successful families do something in addition to good financial and estate planning. They add a third element to their planning.

That element is known today as heritage design. Successful families amplify their good financial and estate planning work by intentionally and diligently passing their stories, values and life lessons to their heirs, along with the money. They focus on building strong communication and trust within the family, and they prepare their family members for both kinds of inheritances that are passed on from one generation to the next—the financial inheritance and the emotional inheritance.

## Two kinds of inheritance

We receive and pass on two kinds of inheritance, not one. The first, the financial inheritance, is the one with which we are most familiar. It is the one around which advisors have built their practices for centuries. But, multiple studies tell us that there is a second, even more important inheritance that we also receive and pass on. That is the emotional inheritance, the sum total of our values, stories, life lessons, and family traditions.

In 2012, a study by the Allianz Company found that leaving a legacy (the emotional inheritance) was far more important to people than leaving a financial inheritance, and that 86% of both "baby boomers" and their parents rated "values and life lessons" as the most important legacy they could receive or leave. Only 10% of boomers said that financial assets or real estate were important as an inheritance. The study concluded that money is a "minor" component of legacy to parents and their heirs. "Many people wrongly assume that the most important issue among families is money and wealth transfer—it's not," said Ken Dychtwald, a gerontologist and survey designer. "What we found was the memories, the stories, the values were 10 times more important to people than the money."

Still, most professional advisors approach planning from a purely financial perspective. "What is your net worth?" "How much money do you want to pass on to your children?" and "How should we plan to minimize your estate taxes?"

To be sure, those questions are important in the context of the professional services that you may need. They always will be important. But, they do not complete the picture. If we have learned anything from decades of experience and studies, it is that planning for the future of your money is not the same as planning for the future of your family. And, when people across the financial worth spectrum define real success in the context of what they want for their children and grandchildren today and for generations to come, money is just about the last thing they mention.

, , ,

The emotional inheritances noted above are different for every person, and unique to every family. In the heritage design process, the advisor helps people to "discover," articulate, share and then utilize what matters most to them as the foundation for all of the financial and estate planning the family will do.

A powerful question

You may have done a great job of financial and estate planning. But, have you also prepared your family for the inheritances they will receive as a result of that planning? Here is a thought exercise that will help to clarify this question: imagine that you could look fifty years into the future, and see your family gathered together in the living room. Now, ask yourself this question: "what would I like to see happening at that gathering, and what would I like to hear them talking about?"

Most people who do this exercise tell us that what they would like to see at that future gathering would be a strong, united family whose individual members are living fulfilling, meaningful and productive lives, involved in the community and supporting and encouraging one another.

What does your vision for such a future gathering of your own family look like? (It is both fun and revealing, by the way, to ask your spouse, children and siblings the same question.) As soon as you have an answer to the big future vision question above, but before you congratulate yourself for what a beautiful image you have conjured in your mind, consider this follow-up question:

How far will the financial and /or estate planning that you have done to this date take your family towards the picture of family harmony, individual accomplishment, community involvement, etc., that you just envisioned when you looked into the future?

Sadly, even people who have done the most artful, complex and comprehensive planning over many years cannot answer that question with much confidence—if they can answer it at all. To be sure, their financial and estate planning will most probably pass their money and other assets successfully to future generations. But what about the tools, training and mentoring that we know, with absolute certainty, are necessary if the heirs are going to be able to effectively use those assets to live the kind of full, productive, family-centric lives that you envisioned in your mind's eye as you looked into the future?

Money is an extraordinarily powerful tool—that, like fire, can be a wonderful servant or a terrible master. Ironically, the better you are at financial and estate planning, the more important it is that you prepare your family for the inheritances (financial and emotional) that they will receive. This is important for all families, no matter their income. It is especially critical for the affluent.

As the Allianz study points out, passing values, life lessons and assuring ongoing family harmony and strength are the most important outcomes that people want from their planning. It is how the "successful 10%" of families avoid the Midas Curse and maintain their family unity and their assets together across generations, through war, depressions and every other kind of economic and political upheaval—including times so rough that today's market and economy roller-coaster look tame by comparison.

, , ,

Heritage design was developed to help families and individuals achieve their dreams across generations. Its underlying principles have nothing to do with money. We have employed our own model of heritage design (via The Heritage Process™) successfully for over two decades as both practitioners and teachers, with families whose estates range from a few hundred thousand to several billion dollars. Heritage design serves people of all income and asset levels well because, as history proves, successfully planning for the future of your money is very different from planning for the future of your family.

The process that we developed to deliver heritage design to families is described below. We will not go into too much technical detail in this book, for two reasons. First, no two families begin, experience or traverse the Heritage Process™ in quite the same way. While the overall principles of the process are the same whether a family goes through the entire six-step process over a period of years, or "drops-in" midway along the chart shown below, the experience itself is customized for each family.

Second, what really matters to individuals and families are the outcomes that they can experience by virtue of engaging in heritage design. What can my family really achieve, people want to know. Can this help to heal some of the long-time rifts that have caused chaos and dissension in the family? How will the unique characteristics, traits, experiences and values that define us now be employed to help us become stronger and more unified in the future? What will doing this mean to us as individuals? What will be different about my family if we do engage in some form of heritage design, compared to what lies ahead if we don't?

Heritage design is focused exclusively on helping you and your family to identify and achieve the things that matter most to you as individuals and as a family, for your reasons. To accomplish that, both the art and the science of heritage design must be applied in equal measure. That is why the methodologies employed by a heritage design professional (or, where feasible, by you alone) to help your unique family achieve the specific multi-generational objectives that you all identify during conversations with your advisors will be unique to your circumstances. Heritage design does not come off the rack in a one-size-fits all box.

Does your family?

, , ,

Mindful of the fact that The Heritage Process™ is just one permutation of heritage design as it is available and practiced both formally and informally around the world, here is a description of the six steps that encompass the complete suite of tools, exercises, activities, products and ongoing meetings that comprise the process we have created over the past two decades to help families at all income levels to beat the Midas Curse. The process is also illustrated below.

### Initial Conversation

During the Initial Conversation (which can be done in a meeting with you, or in a family meeting we call a "Family Forum") we will talk about your vision for you and your family both now and in the future, your current reality (and how close it is to that vision), and The Heritage Process and how it might help your family fulfill your vision. This is an open discussion and a time for you to ask questions, and determine—for your own reasons—whether The Heritage Process is right for you and your family. If you proceed, you will do so at your own pace.

### The Guided Discovery Process™

"Guided Discovery" is a process of learning in which you are guided by another to learn from your own experiences. This journey through your personal treasure chest of memories and life lessons will help you understand yourself and your family as never before, and it will clearly outline the path ahead. The goal of the Guided Discovery interview is to help you identify and articulate your story, life lessons, values, standards and principles. It helps clarify your vision for you and your family both now and in the future, and your concept for a family structure that will facilitate the passing of the family's story, life lessons, values, standards, and principles to future generations. And, it will allow your family to identify and articulate its common vision, and support your family and that vision for multiple generations.

### Heritage Statement

Your Heritage Statement is the documentation of your story and values, combined with the appropriate structure for sharing those values with future generations. In short, it says: "This is who I am. This is where I came from. This is what I believe. This is what I hope for my family, now and in the future." And, it says it in your words, so future generations will hear your story directly from you, and not through word of mouth.

## Collaborative Teams

At some point, your Heritage Statement is provided to all of your advisors, giving them a clear, shared focus for your planning. This helps them to become a dedicated team, working in harmony to align your planning with your goals and beliefs, which will implement your vision now and into the future. This step is not included as part of the main circle on the illustration below, because it can happen any time after your Heritage Statement is drafted.

## Initial Heritage Day

Your family will celebrate its heritage and begin the process of transferring that heritage and preparing your heirs at this special event. At some point during the day, you will share your values, vision and Heritage Statement in an open, honest and comfortable setting. The overall objective of the Heritage Day is to enhance communication in your family and allow your family to experience growth together. We accomplish that through a series of exercises and experiences. The day's activities will strengthen communication in the family, and help begin the gradual transfer of leadership and responsibility to the next generation(s).

## Ongoing Heritage Days

Your Heritage Day marks the moment that you and your family begin to live your heritage-for generations. Families typically develop a family structure and meet at least once a year to have fun and work on the family's activities, ideas, strategies and plans for the future. The purpose of these gatherings is to keep your family unified through active communication, team building, leadership and shared responsibility. This is the time, year after year, where you witness your family working together, making healthy decisions, and nurturing family love and harmony. As shown on the front page graphic, typical themes for the first five meetings are listening, empathy, leadership, personal and family development, and teamwork. However, these themes may vary based upon your family's circumstances.

Heritage design helps to paint the picture that most people envision when they look into the future and answer the question that opened this chapter: what would I like to see if I could witness a gathering of my family 50 years from now? Through heritage design, people can prepare their family to get together, play together, work together and support one another so that each family member has the opportunity to live a fulfilled life.

With heritage design as the foundation for all of the other planning, the family and the assets they have worked so hard to gather can remain strong and unified for generations.

, , ,

What you have been reading about the failure of the inheritance side of the estate planning equation in this book may or may not seem applicable in your life right now. More than one person has taken a look at the concepts of heritage design and asked, "Why should I care about what my children make of themselves? It's their life. Their choice. Let them live with the consequences of the decisions they make. I did."

It's hard to argue with the basic premise of that sentiment. We would be the first to acknowledge that personal responsibility is one of the pillars of a productive life. Whether or not this process is right for you and your family, it is certainly fair to question the underlying philosophy.

But, there is no getting around this fact: whether by design or by default, you will leave a legacy. Some trace of you will remain after you pass. It may be as faint and short-lived as the last snowflake of spring or as strong and enduring as a mountain of granite.

With what degree of impact you bestow that personal legacy on future generations is one of your life's most important decisions.

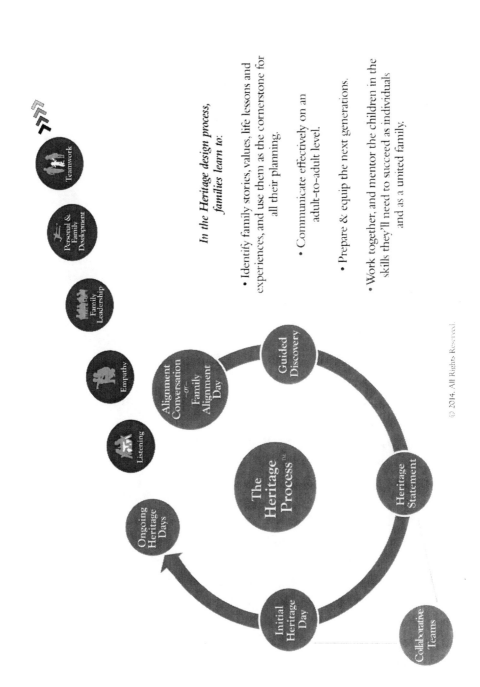

*In the Heritage design process, families learn to:*

- Identify family stories, values, life lessons and experiences, and use them as the cornerstone for all their planning.

- Communicate effectively on an adult-to-adult level.

- Prepare & equip the next generations.

- Work together, and mentor the children in the skills they'll need to succeed as individuals and as a united family.

Teamwork

Personal & Family Development

Family Leadership

Empathy

Listening

Alignment Conversation —or— Family Alignment Day

Guided Discovery

Ongoing Heritage Days

The Heritage Process™

Heritage Statement

Initial Heritage Day

Collaborative Teams

Unfortunately, due to procrastination, lack of time or motivation, or countless other distractions, it is a decision often left up to family members or friends, usually about the time they are picking out a headstone. Take a walk through an old graveyard and look at the weathered basalt columns and ornate decorative stones that mark many of the graves of sturdy, solid citizens whose only enduring legacy resides in that ton or two of solid rock. (The poet Robert Frost once wondered about the *"inverse relationship between the size of the headstone and the size of the legacy."*)

If, like many people, you have asked the question at the head of this chapter, "Why shouldn't my children and grandchildren make something of themselves, just like I did?" we would answer, *they should.* The question then becomes, how did you actually achieve your success? What tools did you have? Who encouraged you, provided you with opportunity, stood beside you, gave you valuable advice? Did you run into any trouble along the way? It could not have been an easy journey. The road to success has more potholes than pots of gold. Was your patience strained, your faith tested? At the end of the day, what was it that sustained you? The answer to these questions contains the perfect description of the true legacy you will leave.

So, we say that if being a self-made, self-motivated, self-reliant individual is an important value to you, one that has been of great benefit to you in your life, then it is also one of the values that can sustain and strengthen your children and grandchildren, just as it did for you. Have you told them? Do they understand what it took for you to get where you are today, in spirit, mind and heart, as well as in bank account? If they don't know the story, how can they ever appreciate the common-sense practical lessons you learned along the road to self-reliance? What will they reach for in their own lives and experiences when they face tough times if they don't have your example upon which to draw?

This line of questions, in a nutshell, explains the thinking behind heritage design. We developed *The Heritage Process*™ in part to help people find an answer to those questions. When we began our work there was nothing like it available for people who sought a structured, effective process to help them craft a significant, lasting legacy. We did not do it to engineer a platform to sell products (we don't sell any), with creative "leave-a-legacy" twists like many of the huge financial houses. Nor to practice psychotherapy. And especially not as a way to provide tools so people could control their heirs from the grave.

, , ,

Our objective was simple: to assist people who wish to pass their values, with their valuables, to the people they love and the causes and organizations in which they believe. Traditional estate planning did not, and could not, achieve those aims. It never will do that successfully, because that is not what it is designed to accomplish.

As we began the long journey of research and development and field-testing, some of our colleagues argued that our plan would never work. Too fuzzy, some said.

Too touchy-feely, another added. Many advisors had ideas, suggestions, reservations, and doubts.

But not one attorney, CPA, planner, or non-profit executive ever said such a process wasn't needed. Nobody took the position that, *"The estate planning system ain't broke, so why fix it?"*

On the contrary. The best, most successful and accomplished advisors in the nation, who between them represent many of the most affluent families in America, all agreed that the traditional system does a wonderful job of passing assets and minimizing taxes, and a terrible job of preparing heirs to receive their material inheritances.

Our task, therefore, was to develop and refine a process that could meet the *show-me* test of the toughest advisors before it could ever be put to work for the clients they represent. It had to be based on solid scholarship, implemented by highly qualified and experienced advisors, and, most of all, it just had to make sense to the families who needed it.

The data, the research and our own experience clearly show that most inheritances fail. Gaining a consensus on that fact was never a challenge—there have never been any takers for the argument that traditional planning builds strong families across generations. But that fact alone wasn't enough to build a new kind of planning model; we had to *redefine* the traditional view of wealth to include more than money and assets. It had to consider the values, virtues and ethics that not only contributed to a client's material success, but also helped make his or her life meaningful and fulfilling.

Next, we had to construct a practical, achievable framework that would promote family strength, unity, and community involvement, while encouraging individual excellence and achievement on the part of family members. Lastly, we had to make the process one which could be taught to, and repeated by, other professionals.

No small feat.

The greatest challenge of all? Learning how to foster an environment within which people would talk to their children about the most taboo, forbidden and mysterious subject in human experience. (No, not sex. That's actually the *second* most hush-hush topic.)

The great forbidden zone of family conversation is nearly always money.

*"There's a toxicity and secrecy around money in many families,"* says Charles Collier, senior philanthropic advisor at Harvard University and author of Wealth and Families. *"As a result, parents fail to provide their kids with any type of financial education—how to invest, say, or how to use a credit card—or to prepare them for the decisions they may have to make about their fortunes. Plus, in many cases, parents are too busy making money and managing their assets to think much about the effect it all will have on the kids."*

As for the contention that 90% of all inheritance problems could be resolved if families just talked about the money, that is true—sort of. Talking about the money in this context does not mean revealing the bottom line on the personal or business balance sheet. It's not about the size of the asset base—it's about what money represents.

Our goal in getting the family talking about money is for them to realize that money is a tool. Just a tool.

A powerful tool, to be sure,but, stripped of its aura of invincibility and curative powers (the "money solves everything" syndrome), money may be seen for what it is: a resource to help strengthen your family through the values you recognize as your most important assets.

With that perspective firmly ingrained your family is freed up to undertake the most significant and rewarding activities of all: working together for the multi-generational benefit of each individual, for the family as a unified whole, and for long-term good of the communities and causes in which you believe.

*Video Break*
Your True Inheritance

**VIDEO: Your True Inheritance**

*Location: Interior / Living Room / Day*

The patriarch and matriarch of the family begin the establishment of new norms with the children regarding their inheritances.

We FADE IN on a family conversation in progress. Present are the family patriarch and matriarch (ages 60+) and their three adult children (two men, one woman, age spans late 20s to mid 30s). The parents' advisor is also present. One son, Matthew, has been estranged from the family for several years. He was going to turn down the advisor's telephone invitation to join in this family meeting until the advisor used the magic words: "We will be discussing your inheritance."
Mom and dad sit together on a small sofa, the advisor sits on a plain chair a few feet away from them. Adult children Sean and Laura share a couch, while their brother Matthew stands, leaning against a wall.

The advisor is speaking to the children:
"It was good to meet you all last night after dinner, even for a minute. I don't always get to meet my client's family… so, this is a rare opportunity. I appreciate you being here."
"This isn't going to be a formal, structured meeting," continues the advisor. "I'm here at your parents' request to facilitate what they hope will be a continuing series of conversations about your family. Your mom and dad aren't taking on that role for two reasons:

first, I told them that in my experience it's best if they can focus on the conversation the same way you will, without also trying to keep an eye on the clock or anything like that. Does that make sense?"

The advisor waits for heads to nod in agreement before he proceeds.

"The second reason I'll be taking on the role of facilitator is that your parents were pretty blunt with me when I asked about the quality of the communication within your family. Basically, they said it stunk. Is that right?"

Sean and Laura don't try to suppress grins when they shake their heads yes. Matthew simply shrugs his shoulders.

"I'll note that as the first agreement we reached today," says the advisor. "Communication in this family is in sore shape. Any objection to me seeing if we can get beyond the 'it stinks' level in our conversation this morning?"

"No objection here," says Laura. "Fine by me," adds Sean.

"Matthew?" says the advisor.

"I'm for whatever will move this along," says Matthew.

The advisor turns to the parents. "Carl, Renee?"

"The higher the level, the better from where I sit," says Carl. Renee nods in agreement.

"Ok," says the advisor. "Then as a family you agree that you are authorizing me to facilitate a conversation that will be positive, respectful and forward-looking.

Today is all about where this family is going—not about where it's been. Everybody onboard?"

Everyone nods in assent.

The advisor sips his coffee. "Good. How about we begin our conversation with a question or two? For starters, what is your understanding for the purpose of our meeting here today? Laura? Would you mind sharing your thoughts?"

Laura seems a little uncomfortable with the question. Her parents are well-off financially, but she hasn't had a very close relationship with them for some time. Being asked to openly acknowledge in their presence that she is there to talk about their money isn't easy.

"Well, as I understand it, we're here to talk about mom and dad's estate, and the inheritance plans they have for Sean and Matthew and me," she says. "That's how I… that's what I think we're doing."

"Sean, how about you… our purpose today?" says the advisor.

"Pretty much what Laura said, I suppose…mom and dad want to tell us about our inheritance," says Sean.

"Original," Laura says to Sean.

"Just saying it like it is," replies Sean.

"And what about you, Matthew?" asks the advisor.

"I was invited to come here to talk about my inheritance," says Matthew. He turns his palms out at his side. "That's all." He doesn't have to add: "you dummy." His tone implies the words.

"We are all in agreement as to our purpose today?" the advisor asks the parents.

Mom nods and says, "Yes, I believe we are."

Dad looks at the advisor as if seeking approval for what he is about to say. The advisor nods for him to proceed.

"That is our purpose, exactly," dad says. "But to make sure that we are all just as clear as can be during this pow-wow of ours, I'd like to suggest that we each also define what the term 'inheritance' means to us individually."

The advisor opens his hands as an invitation to anyone who wants to speak.

"Well, it's the money," blurts Sean. His lightning-fast response earns a laugh from Laura and Matthew. Sean is a bit embarrassed.

Laura is feeling a little bolder, especially after Sean's unguarded remark.

"I guess I think of money when I hear the word inheritance, too," she says. "I mean, that's what parents do, right? They leave their money to their children when they die."

"My big brother is a little quick on the draw, but he got it right," says Matthew. "Inheritance means money. The cash, the property, investments. Real assets. The stuff that has value, that… the stuff that matters."

The advisor sets his coffee down. "So you are in agreement on that point: for each of you, your inheritance means the money you will receive from mom and dad. Period."

The three children look at one another. "Well, yeah, of course" says Matthew. "It's like a rite of passage for families, isn't it? Dad and mom sure can't use the money after they're gone… unless dad has that one covered, too."

The father shakes his head. "I have no plans to take it with me, Matt."

"You can rest easy about that."

Matt looks pleased with himself for having scored a point against his father. The advisor moves on: "Renee, we haven't heard much from you this morning. Would you like to tell us what the term 'inheritance' means to you?"

Mom clearly feels a little awkward in this forum. Her hands have been in her lap, and she has mostly been staring at the floor. At the advisor's question she unfolds her hands and takes her husband's hand in hers. She looks at the advisor, and then at her children. We see love in her eyes, but we also see pain and regret at the state of the family's relationship.

"Here is what I believe…," she begins in a soft voice.

Sean interrupts: "Mom, could you please talk a little louder?"

Mom clears her throat, and begins again. "What 'inheritance' means to me. You know, it wasn't so long ago that I would have agreed with the definition you three just used. Inheritance is money. I know that's how most people think of it. But there is more, so much more that inheritance really means… at least to me."

It is clear from the expressions on the children's faces that there haven't been many times in their lives when their mother spoke from her heart. Even Matthew's countenance softens as his mom continues.

"A minute ago, Matthew, you said that inheritance is about the stuff that matters," she says. "You are more right about that than you know. Where you and I part company, though, is on the definition of the things that really do matter, the things that are so important to each of us as individuals and as a family that we want to preserve them and cherish them and guard them in every way we can so that we can hand them to our children and grandchildren someday just as perfect as they were when we received them. "

Mom lowers her gaze a moment in reflection. Then she raises her head and continues. "When your father and I got married we had nothing. We lived in a rented room behind a feed store for the first year, until your father was able to save enough for us to rent a little house. You were born soon after we moved in, Sean. Dad worked 12 hours a day, 6 days a week for several years. We scrimped and saved and set aside everything we could for a down payment on our first business. Dad jokes that I used to take the bus across town to save a nickel on a can of peas. That's true, except for the bus part. I actually walked the mile to do my grocery shopping at a better store than the one in our neighborhood."

"We had absolutely nothing in the way of material comforts. Hand me down furniture, no car, and when you three came along I even sewed your clothing so that we could save a little more."

Mom pauses a moment, and reaches to a side table for a tissue. She dabs her eyes before going on.

"My mother died just 2 weeks after you were born, Laura. She got to see you, I was always grateful for that. My father died when I was 3, so I didn't know him. Mom lived in a small apartment, just her and a mean old cat.

She had no money or property or investments.

"In fact, my total inheritance of 'stuff' from her consisted of a worn-out Bible, an album of old family pictures, and her wedding ring. Wherever we have lived, those three things have always been on their own little shelf in the living room. Next to my pictures of each of you, those are my most treasured possessions."

"By the time Matthew was born, we had opened our first office.

We bought a house. One office became another and another and then another…well, you all know that part of the story. What you don't know, though, is that the happiest days in my life were those early days when every day was a struggle.. We had each other, we had our dreams, we had three healthy babies… so, all this? …" she waves her hand at the beautiful furnished room in which they are sitting "… doesn't compare to how rich I felt when we lived in that leaky little house on Broad Street."

Mom sighs, and dabs here eyes once more.

"Anyway," she says, "to me, an inheritance is anything that you receive from someone dear to you that helps you to be a better person… something that someday, when your own time comes, you can pass along to those who have been dear to you."

Laura smiles softly at her mother when she is done speaking. Sean is reflective, and Matthew is staring down at the floor. No one speaks.

"Well I didn't mean to hush you all up," mom says. Everyone chuckles at that—even Matthew.

"Carl, you began this conversation about inheritance," says the advisor.

"Everyone else has shared their thoughts about what inheritance means. It's your turn."

Carl is a strong, forceful personality, even when sitting quietly on a chair. When called upon, he addresses large groups of his employees in a booming voice that carries to the back of the warehouse. It is a 'commanding presence' that his children witnessed first-hand in their home for years, and it is what they expect to see from their father today.

So, when Carl begins to speak in a voice so quiet and deliberate that the children have to lean forward to hear him, it is a new—and surprising—experience for them.

"A few weeks after my dad died, my brothers and I were asked to come down to the attorney's office for the reading of his will. I was 36, and your mother and I had just opened our third store. Dad was a pipe-fitter, and there wasn't much in the way of an estate. It was a pretty cut and dried business: the lawyer read the legal jargon, including how dad wished his assets to be distributed. Afterwards, my brothers and I went to a local pub and had ourselves a few drinks in honor of the old boy."

As Carl speaks, Matthew edges away from his spot against the wall and joins his brother and sister on the couch.

"I remember thinking as I drove home that night," Carl continues. "Is that all there was to it? Inheritance, I mean. Can a man's whole life be distilled down to 4 or 5 pages of 'whereas' and 'hereto' and 'now therefore?'"

"My dad was a stand up guy. He was a hard worker who loved his family and his friends.

He loved to read history. And he loved to fish. Was a pretty good harmonica player, too, and in a pinch he could knock out a fair ragtime on the piano. He taught my brothers and I to love our country, to respect the law, to share our good fortune with people in need, and he even tried to teach us not to take ourselves too seriously."

All three children try to muffle laughs at that comment.

"Yeah, I know," says Carl. "He didn't do such a good job with me on that one."

"What I was sure of when I walked out of that lawyer's office," Carl continues, "was that the Last Will and Testament he read that day in no way, shape or form had anything to do with the true inheritance dad had passed to his sons. That inheritance was something deeper, something more meaningful, something that was going to outlast any money or possessions we were getting."

"And that thought has always been in the back of my mind over the years. Tell you the truth, though, I never did anything concrete about it, I didn't know how to, or even if the idea of somehow writing something down that represented the real inheritance I received from my dad was even possible."

"But I never let the idea go, either. So when your mom and I engaged Jeffrey to help with our estate planning, one of the first challenges I gave him was to help us to discover a way for mom and me to communicate with you and your children about the things that have mattered most in our lives, the things that mean more to us than the money. The real inheritance we want each of you to have and to someday share with your children."

The expressions on the children's faces range from a little puzzled (Laura), to a bit uncertain (Sean), to a growing sense of apprehension that some really bad news is about to hit the fan (Matthew).

"I knew this wasn't what the three of you expected to be talking about today before we began this conversation, but after hearing each of you describe your ideas about what an inheritance is, I'm more convinced than ever that this is something really important for our family to talk about."

"Jeffrey gave mom and I the idea when he suggested that if we really wanted to invite you three to help us to find a new way for our family to communicate about the things that truly matter, that we might want to start by... how did you describe it Jeff?"

"By taking the risk off the table," said the advisor. "By starting a conversation that takes the money out of the mix for the time being so that you can talk about another kind of inheritance, your family's emotional inheritance. All of the values that you hold dear as a family and as individuals, your traditions, stories, life lessons... all of the things that actually define you as a family."

The children share expressions that are a mix of surprise and disbelief. Their Type-A, driven father is inviting them to participate in a conversation about emotional matters?

Matthew is the first to speak. His tone is more
one of genuine puzzlement than disrespect:
"And this conversation about our emotional
inheritance is supposed to take us where,
exactly?"

Carl breaks out with his first big smile of the
day.

The advisor speaks. "That destination is
entirely up to you as a family. You'll only
get there if you each commit to helping one
another along the way. You won't get there
this morning, and there's sure to be some
bumps along the way as you lay out the path
ahead. How well this all works out will be
determined by the way each of you deals with
two questions: Can you do it? And, is it worth
it to you to engage in the process? Your mom
and dad have answered yes to those questions.
That's why they are here today. My job is to
keep the process on track as you discover what
this whole inheritance idea means to you as a
family."

Laura says, "And how will we know if this
process is working?"

"From where I sit," says the advisor, "it
already is."

As the parents and children continue talking,
we FADE OUT.

-end-

# CHAPTER SEVEN

## Sustaining Family Wealth & Unity for Multiple Generations
*"One generation plants a tree, the next generations enjoy the shade."* Anon

The most important conclusion we reached in our years of research about the Midas Curse was this: your own family's assets, and its strength and unity, can be successfully sustained from one generation to the next. The specific elements required to accomplish this have been tried, tested and proven over centuries. History, culture, politics, geography—none of these are critical factors in determining whether a family will succeed or fail across generations.

We know that to be true because for as far back in time as we can look, the records show that families who have remained strong and unified generation after generation share certain traits and characteristics in common that transcend cultural, economic and political boundaries.

The traits that have sustained the Kikkoman soy sauce family of Japan since they launched their business in1603, for example, are little different from the traits that have helped Europe's Rothschild banking and investment family remain strong and untied for over 200 years, or America's Kennedy family since the 1920's.

However, an appreciation for the traits that successful multi-generational families share in common have only recently begun to sink into the consciousness of the mainstream planning professions. In our own individual practices we have seen the 90% Midas Curse failure rate hit family after family, including families who were not just clients, but also close friends. Our research focused not on finding the causes of family implosion (those are all too easy to explain!), but by a desire to understand how to help all families become stronger and more united today—and to stay that way. Thus, the central question we asked was: "if 90% of families fail to keep their unity and their assets together across generations, what do the 'successful' 10% do differently?"

We knew that if we could discover identifiable behaviors, traits and characteristics (if any) that successful multi-generational families shared, we could distill those "elements" into tangible tools and processes that could be used to help all families grow and stay strong for multiple generations.

, , ,

Our ongoing work, bolstered by a growing body of contemporary studies and the cumulative experience of professional advisors around the world, provided the answers that we sought. Families who remain strong and unified across generations do indeed share certain important elements in common. In fact, they share about a dozen "elements of success" in common, including how they intentionally teach and transmit those elements to succeeding generations.

Before we examine those elements, though, we want to reinforce an important point: it is clear from the historical evidence, studies and anecdotal advisor experience that there is no relationship whatsoever between the amount of money a family has and its ability to apply these elements successfully in their own circumstance. Sustaining wealth and unity across generations, as it turns out, is less about money than it is about preparation and intentional action.

## Background

Whatever the characteristics that distinguish one family from another, from culture to family stories, educational attainment or net worth, the kinds of things that most parents want to pass on to their children share much in common. It is a basic human desire to want to pass not just what we have (our assets) but also who we are (our stories, values, life lessons and experiences).

From a historical perspective it is clear that the successful 10% achieve multi-generational unity and prosperity less because of the success of their financial and estate planning than from the fact that they have integrated some level of heritage design into their lives.

Each of the primary elements that comprise heritage design (from the informal, do-it-yourself variety to more formal advisor-guided activities), and the process by which they can be customized to reflect your family's unique circumstances, is described individually below. In practice (inside a planning process that brings all of the elements together), there is not a rigid, one-size-fits-all heritage design path. The elements can be integrated into your life and family experience in ways that are truly your own. Over time, any process your family creates, internalizes and passes from one generation to the next to sustain its wealth and unity across generations simply becomes a reflection of who you are and what you routinely do as a family.

## Elements for Sustaining Family Wealth & Unity
## Element I

*Foster strong and effective communication,*
*and build trust between generations*

Earlier in this book we referenced the Family Office Exchange, the national organization that provides professional advising services to family offices. Their perceived risk study asked clients, "What are the most critical risks facing your family?" (Essentially—what will get you?) To no one's surprise, the vast majority of the respondents cited poor planning and investments as the most likely potential culprits. Just 7% perceived family dynamics as a possible risk factor.

Unfortunately, as we have seen, this is one of those instances where the conventional wisdom had it all wrong. The Williams and Preisser study we detailed earlier reported that 60% of the more than 2,000 families who really did lose their assets and their unity said that it was lack of communication and trust in the family that brought about their demise. 25% said their troubles were caused because of unprepared heirs. Amazingly (at least as far as conventional wisdom goes), less than 3% of the respondents in this comprehensive study said that financial issues like poor planning and investments had brought about their wealth loss.

The wildly divergent conclusions of the two studies above underscore the knowledge gap between the factors that conventional wisdom say are the causes of lost assets and family unity versus what actually happens in real life. The Williams and Preisser study in particular supports the conclusion that building and enhancing trust and facilitating effective communication within the family are foundational to family success.

And that communication must be "adult-to-adult," meaning adult children or grandchildren must be able to express themselves as adults, even when speaking to their parents or grandparents. To accomplish that, zones of safety and trust must be created in the family communication process. The keys to doing this successfully have come to be known as the "3 P's" (so-named by Buchholz and Roth in their book, Creating The High-Performance Team). The three P's are:

### Permission.
All individual family members need to be given permission to assert themselves and take the first step.

### Protection.
All family members need to feel safe in asserting themselves.

### Potency.
All family members need to feel that what they contribute will make a difference.

A trained facilitator can set the stage for utilizing the 3 P's effectively in family meetings. Heritage design in this context bridges the gap between perception (thinking that poor planning and investments will get me) and reality (if I want to keep my family and my assets together for generations, I need to begin with communication and trust). In part, heritage design does this by providing the family with training, tools and mentoring that have been proven to enhance multi-generational communication and trust.

, , ,

## Element II
*Develop, maintain and regularly re-visit your vision for the present & the future.*

A clear, well-defined statement of the family's vision for the present and the future is a core characteristic shared by successful families. It may be as simple as a family crest or motto, or as long as a written history of the family that is updated by each generation. Heritage design uses such statements—however they may be ultimately expressed— as the source for the inspiration, direction, planning and inter-family education that will help preserve and strengthen the family and its assets from generation to generation.

Great significance is given to the development of that vision and to the way it is expressed and shared with the family. In its written form, this statement is often referred to as the family's Heritage Statement. In this statement, the values, stories, history, life lessons, experiences, hopes and dreams of the generation who creates it are provided as a "pre-inheritance" resource and guide to the generations who will follow.

The articulation of this vision by one generation is not cast in concrete, sacred and immutable. Far from it. The statement and the vision underlying it should be revisited by future generations as a reference point for understanding how the family has made both their financial and non-financial decisions, but at the same time each new generation should update the Heritage Statement to include additions to the family story and life lessons.

In whatever form it may take, from a written document of a few pages to an actual book about the family, or a video or audio recording, we can assure you that when you find a family who has remained unified and strong for generations, you will find a family who has a clearly defined, shared vision that is intentionally passed from one generation to the next.

,,,

## Element III
*Successful families meet regularly.*

Wealth and tradition can only be transferred successfully inside a family that is unified. A united family is forged by common bonds of family history and family experience. One of the best ways for families to experience and share those common bonds is by holding regular Family Meetings. Typically these get togethers revolve around three major activities:

**Family Fun**
**Family Development**
**The Business of Being a Family**

*Family Fun* — The title speaks for itself; these are shared activities from games to sports to vacations; this is time for your family to be itself and to simply enjoy one another's company.

*Family Development* — The possibilities here are endless when planning for the unique needs and interests within your family. For example: You may have guest speakers from the worlds of business, the arts, philanthropy, or other fields of interest and inspiration. Family and marriage counselors may share strategies for building strong families. Or career guidance specialists may meet with high school and college age children, establishing mentoring teams within the family. These are just a few ideas, but your family dynamic will reveal events and activities that would most benefit your unique needs.

*The Business of Being a Family* — This activity must be separate and distinct from any business or investments the family may own. The business of the family focuses on activities and projects that you select and undertake as a way of inspiring individual family member achievement while building family unity and a common family vision. That's not to say that family investments, businesses or philanthropy cannot be discussed in this forum.

However, the family must not lose sight of the larger objective for this activity, and that is the recognition and development of everything that binds you as a family. Conversations about the business of being a family will range far beyond issues of money. Plus, children will get to see their parents involved in some activities as equal participants, not as facilitators or leaders.

Planning, setting up and helping to facilitate the first few annual meetings is typically done in conjunction with a professional who is trained to help structure and guide the event to reflect your unique family situation. However, there are many aspects of the family meeting that you and your family can plan for and manage without professional guidance.

, , ,

### Element IV
*Promote a balanced definition of the meaning of "Wealth."*

Ask any ten people to define "wealth," and you will probably get as many different answers. (Many will have something to do with financial wealth, including property, investments, cash, etc.) In the broader scope of things, and in particular as it relates to the idea of the successful transfer of wealth and unity from one generation to the next, there are four generally accepted definitions of wealth that we must consider. As described by Jay Hughes, author of *Family Wealth: Keeping It In The Family,* they are:

**Human Capital**
This wealth is comprised of your family, health, backgrounds, talents and attitudes.
**Intellectual Capital**
This wealth includes formal and informal education, work ethic, spiritual life, family stories and life lessons.
**Social Capital.**
Includes citizenship, philanthropy and volunteer work.
**Financial Capital**
The family's financial wealth includes all of its personal property.

With this more encompassing definition of wealth in mind, consider how this show-stopper would go over at your next family meeting: when all the children (grandchildren, too) are assembled and quiet, tell them: "I have some good news: we're going to talk about the most important inheritance you will ever receive." [Note: you will be able to hear a pin drop about now.]

At this point you will have their attention. You can then describe how throughout history one of the characteristics that successful families have shared is a "proper" relationship with money, and an understanding that true wealth is far more than material assets. Your life has been filled with a wealth of lessons and experiences that, when intentionally shared with your children, may become the most valuable assets they possess. This is a wonderful way to share that lesson.

Families who are able to sustain their wealth and unity from generation to generation define the money as a tool, best used to achieve the things that really matter. What kinds of things? They're different for every family, and typically reflect the vision and values that the family has identified as part of their core identity. What's important to note is that we receive and pass on two kinds of inheritances, not just one. We all know about the first inheritance, the money. But, we also receive an emotional inheritance, which is the sum total of those values, life lessons, stories and experiences we have discussed. If we don't understand our emotional inheritance, history tells us that there is a 90% probability that we will squander our financial inheritance. That's why preparing your heirs to receive both of their inheritances is so important.

, , ,

**Element V**
*Keep the family business (including investments) separate from the business of being a family.*

If your family owns a business or manages family investments, you know that family get togethers are often dominated by conversations that center on the business' operations. There is a place—an important place—for talk about your business, but it should not interfere with or compete with the other purposes of your family. The ideal is that everyone understands that while you are a family that owns a business, you are not a business that owns a family.

We have been told by adult family members who are not part of the family business that they never really felt like they were a contributing member of the family until they had the chance to participate in the kinds of family structures (like Family Councils or family assemblies) that heritage design makes possible. Every family member may not be suited to play a significant role in a family business or investments, but they should still be honored as a valued family member. The way your "business of being a family" meetings are structured and operated will eventually create new family norms, including the value and enjoyment of working together, of maintaining family harmony, and of always working on something as a family.

Keeping the family business separate from the business of being a family has been a key ingredient of successful wealth and unity transfer for centuries. It allows the family and the family business to succeed on their own as separate entities.

, , ,

## Element VI
*Identify the roles necessary for the family to be successful (non-financially as well as financially).*

Each generation within your family needs to know what roles must be fulfilled if the family is to be successful. In many families, individuals take for granted that things just somehow get done, as if by magic. Consider adult children who have signed tax returns related to their trusts for years, but don't understand the accounting, investments or other issues behind the returns. Or the college student who suspects—but isn't positive— that there is some kind of relationship between her parents leaving the house every morning at 6:00 AM and her tuition getting paid.

There are a host of business, financial and legal issues that directly impact the family about which many children (even 50-year-old children!) simply have no clue. To understand these issues and activities is to understand the roles played by the family members and professionals who create and manage them. It is also one of the ways in which children are able to identify and fulfill important roles within the family themselves. (Those roles can be as simple as helping keep track of who is coming to the next family gathering, to more complex roles like helping manage the family bank. The point is, everyone in the family has the opportunity to contribute in meaningful ways.)

A common theme among the 90% of families who are unable to "keep it together" from one generation to the next is that the vital roles that keep things humming are either misunderstood or are a complete mystery to the children and grandchildren.

Young children learn about roles within the family through observation. Adult children can understand and identify the roles of their various family members. (We recognize that there may be instances where special needs, disabilities or personal struggles can make this difficult, and require some family members to take on care-giving and assistance roles.) The goal is for there to be open, honest communication about how and why individuals chose their roles, and what value those roles contribute to the family. When that occurs, mysteries about "magic ATM's" with their boundless cash and documents that appear from thin air will disappear.

In heritage design, the differences that exist within your family are viewed as one of its greatest sources of strength and enduring, dynamic flexibility. No matter what the interests and abilities of any individual family member may be, there are usually ways to find opportunities for them to participate (under the guidance of professional advisors or other family mentors) at some level in financial decision-making. In other words, everyone has a role to play.

, , ,

### Element VII
*Inspire individual family members to participate – for their own individual reasons.*

Individual family members must be prepared to receive their emotional as well as their financial inheritance.

Furthermore, each person must decide, for their own reasons, to participate in the kinds of family events and activities described in this article.

We call this decision-making process the "Is it worth it? Can I do it? conversation.

In our experience, it will be "worth it" to individual family members only if the family truly values each individual voice. It also helps when the family supports each member to find a meaningful and productive role within the family structure for the expression of their core passions. Of course, for some it may be worth it if there is enough money at stake to compel them to participate.

The process by which individuals make the decision to participate for their own reasons is easier to undertake if they have a strong grounding in understanding the various roles necessary for overall family success (as described above), and if they—and their family—are enthusiastic and supportive about the roles they have chosen for themselves.

, , ,

### Element VIII
*Train and mentor each generation.*

Individual family members who understand, embrace and are capable of executing their current and future roles within the family and its financial welfare will find that it is worth it and that they can do it. The mindset, education and skills necessary for them to perform their roles can come from many sources, including mentoring.

Mentoring for success is a hallmark characteristic of families who successfully sustain their wealth and unity. Mentoring can take place in many arenas; in the area of philanthropy it can provide opportunity for the children to learn about the power and impact of giving, and how and why the parents have selected the organizations they support and the difference their giving has made in the world. In the area of business and finance, mentoring can involve the children investing and spending real money to learn real-world skills, decision-making processes and lessons.

We call these kinds of activities Pre-Inheritance Experiences. They prepare the children for the real responsibilities they will take on later in life, and they can be accomplished in "small bites", with relatively small amounts of money and authority being given to the children in the next generation — no matter how old they may be. Parents, grandparents, aunts and/or uncles may mentor on important business or investing principles that built the family business or investments that contributed to the success they now enjoy. This may also include preparing the next generation to take over the family business.

A key that we have found in beginning any mentoring relationship is to focus on process before performance. That way, the focus of the mentor (particularly if it is a parent) can be on the process (how to save, how to invest, how to budget, etc.) rather than on the performance. Plus, focusing on process allows the children to make mistakes, and to learn from those mistakes without their actions adversely impacting the family. Overall, children learn a far better lesson with the question "describe what you learned with the money you worked with," than, "tell me what you earned with the money you worked with?"

The law of consequences still applies, and lessons aplenty are still learned in a mentoring process like this, but often very little money needs to be spent. Pre-Inheritance experiences are often the most effective way to mentor, train and establish decision-making processes for successive generations.

Mentoring of individual family members can also be done by outside professional advisors. This may be particularly effective where "gaps" exist where there is an essential role that needs to be filled but no family member is equipped to take it on.

, , ,

## Element IX

*Facilitate the genuine transfer of leadership from generation to generation.*

There may be no more misunderstood (and/or even feared) element required for the successful transfer of wealth and unity in families than that of the transference of leadership from one generation to the next. For some patriarchs and matriarchs, the mere words "leadership transfer" suggest loss of control, influence and decision-making authority. And yet, the process by which leadership skills are developed and transferred is the cornerstone of the successful multi-generational family.

Transferring leadership within the family is ultimately not about what the parents give up, but what they gain. When every family member at every level can participate and contribute to the business of being a family in a manner with which they feel comfortable (up to and including NOT having to assume leadership positions if they don't wish to), the entire family benefits now and in the future. A key to the transfer process is this: when individual family members have identified, prepared for and are capable of executing the roles they have chosen to play within the family, they must be invited to begin taking on leadership roles. Effective leadership transfer takes place intentionally. It does not happen by accident or by chance.

A family in which the interests and contributions of the carpenter are as valued and important to the family as those of the CEO of the family business, the artist, the student, the attorney, the teacher and the stay-at-home parent is a family that can weather any storm. Also, it's important to remember that there can be many kinds of leaders in a family, including those who have nothing to do with business or money.

An example of this "other" kind of leadership could be the strong grandmother who in every way, shape and form is the keeper of family traditions, family holiday schedules, vacation planning, etc. Each generation needs a CEO of the family just as it needs a CEO of the business. They may be the same person. Often, they are not.

Each generation must develop its own leadership, or unity and wealth will be lost. There are simply too many elements needed to keep a family and its finances together for more than one generation to succeed in the absence of strong leadership. Families can either get lucky enough to have strong leadership simply "appear" in each generation (a very rare occurrence in our experience), or leadership skills can be modeled, mentored and passed intentionally.

Families who develop leadership in each succeeding generation are able to pass the torch by the handle, rather than by the flame.

, , ,

## Element X
*Require true collaboration between your professional advisors.*

When was the last time that all of the professional advisors who work on your behalf got together in the same room to talk just about you? Our experience is that unless you have a Family Office, the answer is never, even for families with very large estates.

Preparing and implementing all of the various plans, products, services, ongoing review and adjustment of your unique plan will not be accomplished by a single individual. Instead, a team of professionals from different disciplines will take on these tasks. That team, with expertise in fields ranging from accounting and law to investing and insurance, will be an integral part not just of your planning, but in a very real sense, an integral part of your life.

Sadly, effective and interdependent team collaboration of this kind is still a rare occurrence in the planning world. Communication between financial, legal and other professionals during the planning and implementation of most plans is typically achieved via e-mail, fax, phone and brief face-to-face meetings. Basically, each professional works in his or her own "silo," communicating only when asked to provided data.

That is not collaborative teamwork.

One of the hallmarks of good heritage design is the selection of the advisors who will work as a fully collaborative team on your behalf. This element is critical for effectively sustaining wealth and unity from generation to generation. Your fully collaborative team should work together creatively, considering all of the alternatives available, and agreeing together on the recommendations for you and your family. And after you have made your decisions from among the options presented, your team should go to work together on implementation, ongoing review, administration and compliance to make sure the plan really will achieve the outcomes that you want. It is possible, and you should expect this level of service.

(See Collaborative Teams in the Appendix for more detail on what you should look for from your own fully collaborative team.)

Assembling a fully collaborative team is not just a one-time job, by the way. Heirs must be trained how to build an effective team so that the planning team itself becomes a multi-generational resource to your children, grandchildren and beyond. Teaching how to interview professionals, and what to expect from professional relationships will help future generations of your family maintain the highest level of professional support.

, , ,

### Element XI
*Create mechanisms for ongoing family governance.*

Each of the elements required for successful transfer of family wealth and unity is valuable in its own way. Each can, on its own, make significant contributions to the overall health and well-being of your family today and for generations to come. History has proven the point.

But there is more to the story. A grocery bag filled with the most expensive ingredients does not magically transform itself into a memorable meal when you set it on the kitchen counter. To prepare a meal that your family will be talking about for years, all of the great food in that brown paper bag has to be cleaned, prepped, cooked and assembled in just the right combination. (Presentation counts, too!) The raw ingredients, as wonderful as each may be on its own, require the application of structure (the recipe) and process (your labor) if they are to become a culinary masterpiece.

It is the same with the various elements we have identified as the required "ingredients" for successfully sustaining wealth and unity from one generation of your family to the next. They must also be shaped within some kind of structure, and developed through the wise application of some kind of specialized process. Historically, successful, enduring families have utilized some form of family governance structure to create and manage all of the elements we have described.

To many the term "family governance" sounds formal, complex and even inconsistent with what a family is supposed to be.

119

However, family governance at its most basic level is merely the process by which a family makes decisions as a group. Great care is taken in the heritage design process to thoughtfully create and launch your initial governance structure.

Conflict is a universal family condition—every family experiences conflict at some point. Many families survive and even prosper despite experiencing significant disputes. The lesson is that it is not the dispute that destroys the family, but rather it is the family's inability to manage the conflict created by the dispute. One of the secrets of effective family governance includes establishing an agreed upon dispute resolution process before a family conflict occurs. When (not if) a dispute arises the family embraces the disagreement in a more relaxed manner and works through the issues using a previously agreed upon process.

Mentoring, supporting, inspiring and motivating each family member, and the family as a whole, can take place within these structures. This is also where pre-inheritance experiences are created that will prepare the children to receive both their financial and their emotional inheritances. The structure of your particular family governance plan may follow some of the models that have been proven over the centuries, but in the end, your governance structure will be as unique as your family. (Learn more about family governance in the appendix.)

⸙ ⸙ ⸙

## Element XII
*Do it now.*

Successful families take decisive action. They pro-actively address each of the elements described in this chapter. They do not put it off, wait for a perfect time, or move ahead only when the waters are calm and the sailing is smooth. ("Smooth waters do not make strong sailors," says the poet.) But, what if one or more of your family members is not "ready" to move ahead with this process? Our friend Tom Rogerson, who has worked with affluent families for several decades, has the answer: "Invite them all, and work with the willing." To be successful, the entire family does not have to be onboard at the launch.

Successful families make a commitment to their vision, and they hold fast to the commitment by putting family first. To be sure, the precise methods, structures and processes they follow may change over time, but when it comes to following through on the fundamental commitments they make to the elements addressed in this chapter, they do not hesitate. They do not waver.

They do not put the business of the family on the backburner even when the storms of depression, recession, political chaos or world war swirl around them. In fact, research shows that in troubled times these families come even closer together. In the face of crisis, they increase the pace, frequency, variety and commitment to their family activities with renewed urgency.

The patriarch of one family with whom we worked put it this way: "There may be bad times to invest in markets, but there is never a bad time to invest in your family." We have seen this philosophy put into action by families who re-allocate or shift existing resources from other activities into creating and sustaining the kinds of activities and structures described here. They take action because they understand that planning for the future of their assets is not the same as planning for the future of their family.

*The lessons of history are unequivocal: to retain both your family unity and your prosperity across generations, the business of being a family must be planned for, tended, supported and celebrated.*

, , ,

According to the Bureau of the Census there are about 114,000,000 separate and distinct households in the Unites States. Each has its own history and its own story. Each has its own traditions, values, hopes and fears. History (the history that we are trying to change) says that only 10% of those families will apply the elements described in this book and achieve multi-generation family success. 90% will not.

It is our hope that an ever increasing number of people will take the elements described here to heart as they think about their family's present circumstance and future goals. You may feel comfortable undertaking some of the elements yourself, without the guidance of a trained advisor. In the case of other elements, there are places where the services of a trained professional are necessary to deliver the best outcomes for you and your family.

If it is your desire to build, maintain and perpetuate your family's wealth and unity across generations, the elements described in this chapter must be implemented—however that best suits your unique situation.

# CHAPTER EIGHT

## Strong by Design

*"We share, to a large extent, one another's fate. We help create those circumstances which favor or challenge us in meeting our objectives and realizing our dreams."* Walt Disney

Nearly 140 years after the last "prairie schooner" rolled across the Great Plains and over the towering Rocky Mountains, you can still see the physical evidence of that pioneer migration, from the wagon wheel ruts lining the hardened clay banks along the Platte River to the names scraped into the face of great red rocks in the Dakota Badlands.

The trek West was a uniquely American experience; a harrowing journey from poverty to opportunity, a new start for anyone strong enough and brave enough and stubborn enough to stand up against every kind of calamity and hardship that nature and man could throw at them.

In the Spring of 1871, one of those wagons carried a young medical doctor, his wife, teenage daughter, and every possession they owned. Dr. Phillip Granger was headed for Eastern Washington, where he planned to open a general practice in a tiny farming community in Palouse County. According to his diary, Granger pulled into the tiny hamlet of Palouse on July 12th with only $81 to his name. The next morning he sold his wagon and team of horses, rented an empty house at the end of the town's only street, and hand-painted a sign that read: P. Granger, Physician & Surgeon, Now Open. The sign was dry enough to hang out front by 1:00 that afternoon, and Dr. Granger saw his first walk-in patient at 1:30, before his wife and daughter had finished unpacking his medical instruments.

, , ,

139 years later, almost to the day, Rod stood on a bluff overlooking the town (which to this day has only a few hundred residents) with Philip Granger's great-great-grandson, Lawrence Granger.

Six months earlier, Lawrence had engaged Rod to guide the Granger family through the Heritage Process™. They were up on the bluff to talk about Lawrence's family history, and in particular, about the values, traits, experiences and sense of unity that were the cornerstone of everything the family valued.

Below them, a rail car was being loaded from one of the three towering grain elevators that were built by Lawrence's family in 1907. As far as the eye could see, fields of hard red spring wheat shimmered in the afternoon sun. Harvest was just a few weeks away.

Lawrence worked at the elevator through high school, and during summers in college. Alongside him worked his uncles, cousins, brothers and sister. His father had worked there, too, before going to law school and taking on a leading role in managing the family's growing business concerns that by 2010 included not only the elevators, but wheat farms, a seed and fertilizer operation, real estate, research and development, a venture capital arm, and banking.

Lawrence described the role that his grandmother and mother had played in not just helping to build the businesses (while raising families) but also in taking on pioneering roles with their local and state school boards and as hospital and college foundation trustees.

"I can't remember my mother ever not being involved in something that could help the community and our state," said Lawrence. "If she wasn't rushing out the door to go to a local fire district meeting she was on the phone raising money for new programs at the state university."

"Being involved in the community wasn't some highfalutin ideal my parents preached—they practiced it day in and day out. Same with my uncles and cousins and their families, for as far back as I can remember. Our businesses are built on trusting relationships, and on doing everything we can to make our communities stronger. We've been through some pretty tough times over the years in the farming community. But, we go through those times shoulder-to-shoulder with our customers and neighbors. Those relationships are our most important asset, not our facilities, not our cash. And they're the reason my family stays together, works together, and why we feel good as individuals about what we do every day."

Lawrence had ample opportunity to apply those principles in his own life. Twenty years earlier he had sold his extended family on the idea of investing in a startup software company. It was not an easy decision for them to make, especially since no one in the family had a technology background, and because they had experienced several lean years with other family investments and were not flush with cash.

The family studied Lawrence's plan, they debated and considered and weighed the possible positive and negative impact such a large investment could have on their businesses and their families.

Ultimately, and as a united family they made the decision to fund Lawrence's startup. His software company operated on exactly the same principles of building trust with its customers as did the grain elevator. That commitment was tested when the fledgling company shipped their first major software release only to discover that it had a serious flaw in the code. Hundreds of customers received expensive software that was, for all intents and purposes, useless.

Many business owners would have folded up shop on the spot.

Lawrence did not have deep pockets, and his family had already been financially stretched in providing him with the  start-up capital.

But instead of quitting, Lawrence demonstrated the same stick-to-it gumption that his great-great grandfather displayed when he sold most of his worldly possessions, painted his own open for business sign and stood ready in the parlor for his first patient—and all before lunch, to boot.

Lawrence got in his car and personally visited every customer who had received the buggy software. "You can have your money back if you want it," he said. "I wouldn't blame you for not wanting to do business with us in the future. But, if you'll trust us, and stick with us, I promise that we will fix the problem and we will deliver a software package to you that will pay for itself many times over."

Nearly all of Lawrence's customers took him up on his offer. Ten years later, when Lawrence's company did its initial public stock offering, he invited each of his first customers to a huge BBQ and fireworks celebration on the banks of the river near his home. Two years after that, the unlikely start up funded by family and friends in a tiny farming community had a campus with over 1,000 employees…and was promptly acquired by a software giant for $1 billion dollars.

As they talked on the bluff, Lawrence told Rod that his own teenage children were working at the grain elevator that summer. His son was saving money to buy a used pickup, his daughter was earning cash to go to cheerleader camp. Both also had daily chores around the farm, and both did volunteer work through their church. The fact that their family had a net worth in the hundreds of millions of dollars was far less important to Lawrence than the value that he and the Granger family placed on the trait of individual self-reliance.

"I want to be ready to hand off the reins of leadership before too long," said Lawrence. "And I want my children to have a crystal clear understanding of why the extended Granger family continues to operate by the same values and principles that have guided us since 1871. We have been applying many of the principles of heritage design informally for generations; in fact, I didn't even know there was such a thing until recently. Now we'd like to memorialize our family stories, and values in new ways, and create ongoing Family Governance structures that will allow us to bring even more family members into the process."

, , ,

In part, the heritage design process helps individuals and families discover, identify and articulate what is most important to them, including the stories of where their most cherished values come from. That information is often presented in the form of a Family Heritage Statement, which is shared not only with everyone in the family, but also with their professional advisors so that the planning they do now and in the future will truly reflect the ideals, goals and objectives that matter most to the family.

In the case of the Granger family, the values that had sustained them for over a century came across loud and clear as Lawrence told the family stories. Entrepreneurship. Sacrifice and risk. Trust. Family communication, and the intentional sharing of family stories, life lessons and experiences. Commitment to community. Personal responsibility.

Theirs is a wonderful example of how the "successful 10%" beat the Midas Curse. But it is only one story. In your own unique family circumstance, of course, everything from the stories to the values will be different. It matters not that you don't share the exact values or characteristics of a particular successful multi-generational family, of course. And really, that is the beauty of the heritage design process.

Your own family heritage design process can be as complex as constructing elaborate Family Governance structures under the guidance of a team of professional advisors, or as simple as sharing stories around the Thanksgiving Day table. Your heritage design will be woven from the fabric of your family story. Your experience. Your values, life lessons, hopes and dreams.

Look around you at the dinner table tonight. The "raw materials" necessary to successfully construct and implement a heritage design process for your family are already in place.

*Video Break*
The World Turned Upside Down

**VIDEO: The World Turned Upside Down**

*Location: Interior / Advisor's Office / Day*
We FADE IN as Mark ushers a husband and wife into his office. The man and woman, Thomas and Julie, are in their late 40s. The only things unusual about the well-appointed office are the mini-basketball hoop mounted on one wall, and instead of the ubiquitous advisor's yellow legal pad, computer and folders found on most professional desks, the only items there are 3 piles of $1 bills, arranged in the exact center of the desk. One stack appears to include hundreds of bills, the center stack has 20 or 30 bills, and the third stack is just a few dollar bills high.

Thomas and Julie observe the piles of cash, and share glances that are a mix of bemusement and concern as they get comfortable in the chairs in front of the desk.

"Did we interrupt something important, Mark?" asks Thomas, nodding in the direction of the money.
"Maybe I just wanted to have cab fare handy in case either of you gets a little too uncomfortable with our discussion today and wants to get out fast," replies the advisor as he takes his seat across the desk.
Now the couple share a seriously concerned expression.
"We're here to talk about our estate planning, right Mark?" asks Thomas. "I know we've been dancing around getting started for the past couple of years, but between you and our CPA

and attorney, what's there to be uncomfortable about?"

Thomas picks up the cardboard box he carried with him into the office and sets it on the edge of the desk next to the smallest stack of money. "Our stuff's all here; copies of the bank and portfolio accounts, copies of insurance policies, several years of tax returns, the buy-sell agreements for our business—copies of everything that matters. Now it's time to just apply whatever financial and legal formulas are out there to make sure we've got our ducks lined up so that when Julie and I are gone the kids end up with more of our estate than Uncle Sam gets. Piece of cake for a pro like you… unless we're missing something here?"

The advisor leans back in his chair. "Thomas, Julie," he says, "you are my clients, and you are also my friends. But if that box and what it represents is the be all and end all for the planning you want to do… I'm going to tell you right now that you are missing something. In fact, you're missing just about everything that matters."

Thomas folds his arms across his chest, and Julie looks puzzled. "Mark, I don't understand what you're getting at," she says. She places a hand on the box. "We've spent weeks organizing copies of everything we were told we'd need to get our estate plan together. Trust me, it's all here. Everything you need to construct the plan that's right for us, every document, every contract, every account. Right there on your desk."

"Everything?" says the advisor. He stands up, takes hold of the box and gives it a shake.

"You sure about that?"

Thomas is starting to lose his cool. He unfolds his arms and leans forward. "Look, Mark, if you think we've held something back, or that any of our records won't hold up to scrutiny, just say so. But everybody I know who has done their estate planning has walked into their advisors' office with a box like that, dropped it on the desk, and ended up with an estate plan that satisfies them. Why should we be any different?"

The advisor holds onto the box of records and walks around to the side of his desk. Speaking slowly and deliberately he says, "I know three things: I know that you love your children. I know that you have built a very successful business. And I know that this…" he gives the box another shake,"…won't protect or provide for either of them in the future."

With that the advisor drops the box of records into the wastebasket.

Thomas is out of his chair. He runs one hand through his hair as he says, "That just cuts, it, Mark. I don't know what this performance is supposed to accomplish, but we didn't come here for theatrics. We came for a plan. If that doesn't work for you…"

Julie stands up, and Thomas retrieves the box from the trash. They walk to the door. As Thomas reaches for the door handle, Marks speaks in a calm, tempered voice: "Actually, you don't need a plan, at least not yet. I wouldn't be doing you or your children or your business any favors if I let you put that cart before the horse. Care to know why?"

Thomas and Julie stand in the open door.

Then they turn and walk back over to the desk. But, they do not sit down.

Mark says, "What you have in that box can help us plan for the future of your money. But if you want to plan for the future of your family it won't be of much help."

Thomas holds out the box. "Are you saying we wasted our time and money putting all of this together?" He isn't ready to sit down, but he does want an explanation for what just took place.

"Not at all," says the advisor. "Planning for the transition of the financial portion of your estate is important. And we'll get to it, believe me. But if that…" the advisor points to the box, "is going to drive your planning from here on, then, yes, you would not only be wasting your time and money, but you'd also pretty much be guaranteeing that the assets you have worked so doggone hard to accumulate over the past 25 years will vanish not long after you're gone. And as bad as that will be, the damage that will be done to your children and their families will be even worse."

Mark sits down. He says, "How about we talk?" and motions for Thomas and Julie to join him.

The couple share a long glance, and then take their seats across from the advisor. "Look, Mark, I'm sorry I flew off the handle, but…" Thomas begins.

Mark interrupts him. "But that box represents quite an investment for both of you, doesn't it. Years of struggle and sacrifice to build your business, all that pressure and stress. Hard to believe that all of that work can be boiled down into spreadsheets and financial statements and placed in a single cardboard box."

Julie and Thomas nod in assent.

"I'm not belittling what you have accomplished," says Mark. "But you didn't hire me just to crunch numbers and look for loopholes in the inheritance taxes. When you walked into my office a few weeks ago and told me you were ready to get this planning underway, one of the first things you told me was that you had all kinds of concerns about your children, especially about the impact you feared that inheriting all that money would have on them. Remember?"

"True," says Thomas.

"Jordie is what, 17 now?" says Mark. Is he still having defiance issues and struggling in school?"

"Yes," answers Julie.

"And Clarice just turned 16, she came to my daughter's swim party two weeks ago—in the new convertible you bought her, by the way," continued the advisor. "Pretty nice ride for a teenager."

"Julie, you told me that you were terrified about what would happen if you and Thomas died today and those kids inherited your money and property. Still feel that way?"

Julie nods. "They're not ready, and the truth is that we haven't done very much to get them ready for that eventuality."

Mark smiles. "And yet you came in here today for the express purpose of having me help you to craft an inheritance plan that would have the net result of getting as much of your money as possible past the IRS and right into your children's hands—the very children who you know in your hearts aren't ready to receive all of that cash. Am I the only one here who sees the flaw in that logic?"

Thomas shakes his head and manages a weak smile.

"Touché," says Julie.

"I suppose they'll do as well as anybody else would in the same circumstance," says Thomas.

Mark leans back and throws a mini-basketball he had been holding in his hand across the room. It hits the edge of the backboard, but misses the net. He shrugs.

"Unfortunately," he says, "a couple thousand years of history tell us that even the most sophisticated state-of-the-art planning usually falls on its face when it comes to helping families stay strong and united from one generation to the next."

"A lot of plans fail?" asks Julie.

"Let me put it this way," says Mark. "The three piles of money here? Let's say that the big pile represents what you have accumulated over your lifetimes. Everything you own. Looks pretty nice there…but here's the reality: for as long as records have been kept, about seventy percent of second generation inheritors have blown completely through what their parents earned…"

Mark puts his forearm on the desk and in a sweeping motion pushes the largest pile of cash to the edge of the desk and off into the wastebasket.

Then he holds up the second pile of bills, with just 20 or 30 dollars in it. "And ninety percent of the time what little money the second generation passes to the third generation also ends up disappearing." With that he tosses the second pile into the trash. "The overwhelming odds are that this is about what your grandchildren will have left from your original estate."

Mark picks up the 2 or 3 bills in the remaining pile. He slides those across the desk towards Thomas and Julie.

It's quiet for a moment. Then Thomas says, "That trash can of yours gets a pretty good workout." Mark nods, but says nothing. He is waiting for them to absorb and react to what he just shared.

Finally, Thomas says, "A ninety percent failure rate doesn't speak too highly of the work that you planning pros do for their clients, does it?"

"Actually, when you consider the objectives that most clients tell us they want to achieve when they come to us to get their planning done, I'd say we do a hell of fine job," answers Mark.

"Ninety percent of all inheritance plans fail and you say that advisors are doing a fine job?" says Julie. "That's crazy."

"Based upon years of research and the experience of thousands of my colleagues, a better definition of crazy might be believing that planning for the future of your money is the same as planning for the future of your family," says Mark. "They're not. Sure, we can engineer a plan that will get the bulk of your estate past the tax man and into your children's hands when you both die. That's a textbook definition of successfully planning for the future of your money. And if that's everything that you want your planning to accomplish, we can do that, no problem at all."

"But you just said that ninety percent of all plans fail," says Julie, "families fall apart and they lose the money."

Mark nods. "They do."

"The operation succeeds, but the patient dies," says Thomas with a wry smile.

"In a manner of speaking, yes," says Mark. "Tell you the truth it sometimes mystifies me that most people blindly accept the three generation cycle of boom and bust. One generation makes it, the next generation spends it, and the third generation kisses the last of it goodbye."

Mark lowers his voice, and in a solemn tone says, "It doesn't have to be that way for your family."

"And that's why you threw our files into the trash?" asks Thomas.

"Call it a little incentive to get you and Julie to begin looking at your planning in a new way. A new paradigm, if you will," says Mark.

"Can we start by learning the reasons that most plans fail so we don't make the same mistakes?" says Julie.

"Sure, we can talk about that," says Mark. "There have been all kinds of studies that show how and why people get off track with their planning. But I think there is an even more important question we might want to consider first. If ninety percent of all inheritance plans fail..." he lets his sentence trail off.

Thomas picks up Marks' thought "...then ten percent succeed. Maybe we should be looking at what those families do that helps them to beat the odds rather than worrying about the things that the ninety percent do wrong."

Mark smiles. "Exactly. What specific characteristics and activities do successful families share in common. And by successful, I mean families who stay prosperous and untied generation after generation."

"And you know what those activities and characteristics are?" asks Julie.

"From A to Z," says Mark. "And we can apply that knowledge to help you and your family build a foundation upon which the other parts of your planning..." Mark points to the box containing Thomas and Julie's files..." can be built to last."

Thomas and Julie share a glance. "A new paradigm," says Thomas.

"And a new way of thinking, really" Mark replies. "A new approach to communication within your family, a new way to ask questions, and a new way to explore all of the possibilities for your family's future."

Julie puts her hand on the box of records. "And none of that happens inside here," she says.

"Not yet anyway," says Mark. "That box will have its day, and it will be important, but if what I am hearing from both of you today is that you'd like me to do everything I can to help your family become part of the successful ten percent, that's a journey we'll have to begin from an entirely different place than you've ever experienced."

Mark allows Thomas and Julie to think about that for a moment. Then he asks, "Are you in?"

"Mark, we want the best possible future for our family," says Julie. She turns to her husband: "Honey?"

"I'm all for it," says Thomas. "What do we need to do to get going?"

"Before we move ahead, there are a couple of things that I'm going to ask you to do," says Mark. "First, I'd like to have a conversation about all of the big decisions that you are facing right now in your lives, this one included. I'll ask you to jot them down a little later.

Then, I'm going to ask you to rank those decisions in order from the least urgent to the most urgent. We'll talk about the value you believe you will get in the form of specific outcomes as a result of making each of those decisions. Once you've ranked your decisions and are absolutely clear as to the outcomes you desire, I'll ask you to create a brand new list so that we are all on the same page as to what your most important decisions are and why they are important to you. Our work will begin at the top of your list, with the decision you tell me is the most important one you're facing today."

Mark reaches into his desk and pulls out two yellow writing pads and pens. He slides them across to Thomas and Julie.

"So we start by listing the big decisions we're dealing with right now…," says Julie as she takes up her pen.

"Actually," says Mark, "I'd like to begin with

a preparatory step to help us get clear on the process we're going to follow as we move ahead. OK? Let's talk about how each of you goes about making your big decisions in life individually, and as a couple. That will give us a common frame of reference about the decision-making process you will be using as we move forward. We'll all be on the same page every step of the way."

Thomas looks at his wife. "Sounds like an adventure," he says.

"Is that a good feeling for both of you?" asks Mark.

As Thomas and Julie shake their heads in affirmation, we FADE OUT.

-end-

# CHAPTER NINE

## Discovering What Matters

*If you believe that transmitting the values by which you have lived to succeeding generations is a worthy goal, ask this question "How do you pass on that which has brought you happiness and success?"*

The purpose of heritage design is not to do a psychological or financial makeover of your family to make it look like the Cleaver's in *Leave it to Beaver*. (Heritage design *is not* therapy!) Heritage design helps you first to identify the strengths—including the unique values—that have sustained your journey and enhanced your success. Then it facilitates a process by which you can share your story (and your family's story), your life lessons, and the values, standards and principles by which you live. Finally, the heritage design process creates opportunities (anything from the simplest family traditions to more complex family governance structures) for the family to work and grow together, and it helps them to work with their attorney, CPA, financial planner or other advisors to make sure that their planning reflects their united vision.

However your family engages in heritage design activities, and whether or not you choose to engage a professional advisor who is trained to provide heritage design services, it is important to remember two things: first, heritage design is about what you and your family want to achieve, for *your reasons*. The unique objectives that your family wishes to achieve multi-generationally will be the driver of any planning that you do, not the packages, products or one-size-fits all programs that too often pop out of the advisor's planning microwave.

You and your family will of course choose financial and legal instruments to help you to achieve your objectives. The key here (and the second important point about the process) is that in heritage design the multi-generational course that you and your family chart together will ultimately go way, way beyond planning for the future of the money. In fact, the faster you want to strengthen and unify your family now, and the more that you want that unity to continue for years, the more important it will be to put the assets to work in support of the things that matter most to you as a family—and that kind of preparation will definitely *not* come out of a one-size-fits all bin.

, , ,

Throughout this book we have visited one particular theme many times: the importance of identifying, articulating and sharing what matters most. What matters most to you as an individual, and what matters most to you as a family. In every case study and historical survey we know of going back to the 17<sup>th</sup> century, families who prosper across the years have a crystal clear appreciation for what matters most to them. That appreciation is nurtured, revered, mentored to the young, and intentionally shared by each generation of the family to the next.

That being said, if the multi-generational harmony and prosperity of your family is something that you value, then the single most important thing that you can do for your family right now is to begin your own what matters conversation. You don't need to hire professional advice to do that. You don't have to have a formal family meeting to share what you discovered in your personal "what matters" journey, either.

To illustrate that point, we'd like to introduce you to Martin Forrestal, who is the main character in the novel *What Matters*, by Rod Zeeb and Cameron Thornton. Martin's what matters epiphany was a little unusual, in that it involved a curious moose, but it illustrates just how powerful the search for what matters most can become once you take the first step. This story also includes a very practical exercise that you can do to begin your own what matters list.

, , ,

Martin Forrestal had a problem, bigger by far than the twelve hundred pound bull moose that was banging its antlers against the side of the tent in which Martin was trying to sleep. He shut the sound of his new antlered friend out of his mind, and thought about the events of the past day.

Last night, just a few yards from where Martin and the moose were now making one another's acquaintance, his family was enjoying blackberry cobbler topped with homemade ice cream in the refurbished trapper's cabin where they vacationed each summer.

As they sat around a rough hewn table, Martin's granddaughter Gwen described an assignment her class had been given. It sounded simple enough. Each student was to create a list called: What Matters Most in My Life. "The problem is," Gwen said, "we can't include any things, like toys or computers or ponies. We're supposed to just list the kind of stuff we feel in our hearts. You know, like love, or helping other people, or being good. It's hard." And then, as only an innocent child can do, Gwen dropped a question that would send her granddad outside for some serious personal thinking time.

"Poppa Martin," she asked, "what matters most to you?"

To Martin's surprise, once he had given the obvious answers— the kids, family health and financial security— he found himself stumped. Gwen was right—it was a hard assignment. When you got right down to it, what did matter? He went out back and gathered an armload of seasoned oak and fir, and built a fire in the wood stove. His wife and Gwen settled under down comforters on the couch with a board game and mugs of chamomile tea.

When the fire was going strong, Martin un-boxed the tent he'd bought in town that day, and set it up on the grassy bank of the stream that meandered to within 50 yards of the cabin's front porch.

When the family went to bed, Martin grabbed a pad of paper, a kerosene lantern and a cup of coffee, and settled into a camp chair next to the tent. To his east, just up the mountain slope, was the boundary of a wilderness area that stretched for hundreds of miles. To the north stood a thick forest of blue spruce, and to the south and west an icy-clear stream cut through deep green meadows that were darkening to purple shadows in the last light of day. At the moment, though, the spectacular vista was lost on Martin.

This should be a simple question, he thought. Just two words: what matters. But by the time he had wrestled Gwen's question into some kind of manageable form, the moon was high and bright in the sky, the last wisps of smoke were curling from the cabin chimney, and a cool mist was forming on the surface of the creek.

It was after 1 AM when Martin finally zipped the tent door shut and crawled into his sleeping bag. High above, a carpet of stars blanketed the sky. Next to him was the notepad, filled with his thoughts about what mattered most in his life. He was excited to share it with his family at breakfast. However, about the time first morning light was spilling over the mountain, and the friendly moose was enjoying his first taste of ripstop nylon, Martin woke to realize that while he had cobbled together an important list, he had no idea what to do with it once he had shared it with his family. This was some of the most important thinking he had ever done. It didn't make sense to go through this exercise and then not put the list to some higher purpose on behalf of his family.

Martin sat up, shouted a few times, and waved the yellow pad of paper back and forth outside the tent door. The moose, who wasn't much enjoying the flavor of the tent anyway, grudgingly obliged and splashed back across the creek. Martin went up to the cabin, made a fresh pot of coffee, and sat on the porch as the sun topped the mountain and spread across the meadow. Now that he knew what mattered, what was he going to do about it? The girls would be up soon. He wanted to have his homework ready.

Most of us have had an experience like Martin's (minus the moose, perhaps). A moment when we find ourselves confronted—and confounded—by a seemingly innocuous question that quickly takes us to the core of who we are. Questions like, "Do you love me?" "Why did you make that choice?" "What do you really want?" and "What would you do if you were in my place?" can set us back on our heels, make us scratch our heads, and even lead us to experience some sleepless nights as our own twelve hundred pound moose crashes around in our thoughts. Simple questions stir us the most because the things that matter most in our lives tend to be simple in nature.

Honesty and love, patience and faith, responsibility and family unity, for example, are straightforward, uncomplicated values. Most of us make the intuitive connection between the presence of those values in our world and the quality of life that we lead. But, do you give deliberate and thoughtful consideration to those values, and others, in the ordinary course of day-to-day life?

Perhaps you should. Because when you set out to intentionally discover and then share what matters most to you as an individual, you begin a journey that will challenge you, strengthen you, and bring your family closer together in common purpose than ever before.

, , ,

What would such an outcome look like? Well, think about it this way: do you know the first name of your mother's grandfather? Do you know what he believed in? What he stood for? Would you like your great-grandchildren to know your first name, and what it was that mattered most to you? Do you think those who come after you could benefit from the lessons you have learned, from the truths you have lived by, even from the mistakes you made along the way?

If your answer is yes, how do you plan to make that happen? (For starters, make sure that all of the photos of yourself that are floating around in family albums and computer image files have your name on them!

Your descendants a century from now will at least know your name.) When you begin to think about, and write about, what has mattered in your own life, you launch a powerful process that will grow into a statement to your family and to generations who will follow: who you were, what you believed in, and what you stood for. It is not a will or a contract. It is far more than those documents, important as they are. This is something from which generations of your family can draw strength, meaning, and guidance. It is a legacy.

**How do you get started?**

For all of its outward simplicity, this personal assessment and discovery is no small task. In fact, as you get deeper into it, you may encounter a rogue moose or two of your own.

Begin by "sweeping the decks clear." As you think about your life, and the life you wish for your children and generations of their children, drill down to the unvarnished basics of life, things like character, values, ideals and aspirations. Stay with your objective. Don't be concerned about creating a literary masterpiece—you are creating a list with some supporting detail, not a novel. When your list is complete (the first draft of several, no doubt) and you have identified and articulated what it is that matters most in your life, it is time to ask: what can I do with that information? How can I put it to use to help my family, now and in the future, and even to assist the organizations or causes that I support?

These are important and practical questions. Eventually, the work you begin here may become the foundation for all of your planning. And you can begin this process by yourself, without the assistance of outside advisors. There's a lot to be said for the simplicity of a comfortable chair under the stars with a pencil, a pad of paper, and a cup of coffee (the moose is optional). Either way, with professional guidance or on your own, the goal is the same: to achieve your desired results, based upon your vision, for your reasons.

**Look first to the past**

However you choose to begin thinking and writing about what matters most in your life, it's a good idea to set a few guidelines for your work. When our friend Martin sat down by the river to begin his list, he started with three guiding principles: first, he would limit himself to no more than one or two words to describe each of the things that mattered most in his own life. So, his list began to take shape like this:

*Honor*

*Family Unity*

*Love*

*Responsibility*

*Faith*

*Leadership*

*Philanthropy*

*Forgiveness*

*Compassion*

...and so on.

Once the list was complete, Martin wrote below each word what his own personal definition of that word was. Next, he decided that for each idea or value that he placed on his list, he would also add a sentence or two about where or how that value became important in his life. Who taught it to him? What was it about that person— parent, grandparent, teacher, coach, religious leader, etc.—that had such an impact on him?

Finally, Martin added a "how-am-I-doing" category to his list. For each of the things he identified as mattering most in his own life, he jotted down a few lines about the kind of job he had done communicating that particular value to his family and friends.

The first category, the list of things that mattered most in his life, was tough. Separating the merely important things in his life—like a nice home and a good health insurance plan—from things that truly mattered—like love for his family and giving to his community— was hard work. It took time. The second part, thinking back on the people in his life who taught him or modeled those values, was not just easy, he found, but fun and rewarding.

## Connect the dots

In most cases, Martin had never consciously connected the dots between a particular value he held dear and the person from whom he had learned that value or seen it modeled. Time and again as he thought back on his life, and on the people who had been so important to him, Martin's face broke into a wide grin. And more than once, a memory brought a lump to his throat, especially when he recalled how some of the "ordinary" people in his life had triumphed over extraordinary circumstances by virtue of the values by which they had lived.

When his list was complete, columns one and two were filled with notes. It was at part three of the exercise where Martin's pencil came to a grinding halt. What kind of job had he done communicating to others about the things that mattered most in his life? In fact, he realized, he hadn't even scratched the surface of the myriad ways he could have—and should have—taken the time to deliberately and intentionally share those values with those for whom he cared the most.

If the proverbial eighteen-wheeler barreled down the highway and swatted him out of the game tomorrow, Martin realized, all of the lessons he had learned, all of the great stories he had in his head, in fact, most of the truly important history of his life, would be flattened and lost forever along with him.

## Keeping what matters alive

It is amazing to think about the impact that simple words (the right words!) on just one piece of paper can have upon history. Magna Carta, the Declaration of Independence, the Ten Commandments, and the Bill of Rights are proof positive that the length and complexity of a document have no bearing upon its significance. In fact, the opposite is true. (Consider what your home loan documents would look like piled high on your desk. How does the significance of that skyscraper of paper compare to these two little words: "I do.") When you take upon yourself the wonderful task of creating your own What Matters document, keep that in mind.

**A great way to greet a new year**

Each January, many of us set goals for things we'd like to achieve in the year ahead. We're going to lose weight, shape up our finances, spend more time with our families, maybe even finally get around to putting up some shelves in the garage. A new year means a new start, and for some reason, no matter how briefly it may flicker, there seems to be an extra spark of enthusiasm and commitment in our step in the first weeks of a new year.

If the list of resolutions you made for the year looks a bit lean, consider adding one more. (Of course, it doesn't really matter if today's date is January 2nd, or August 27th or November 14th.)

Find your own quiet place, away from the distractions of work and home. Take pen and pad in hand, and write two simple words in large bold letters on the top of the page:

*What Matters*

The rest is up to you.

*Video Break*
The Empty Table

**VIDEO: The Empty Table**

We FADE IN as a woman in her 50s is finishing up a phone call with her daughter. "I suppose I understand," the woman is saying. "It won't be the same without you and Tom and the kids… yes, I'll tell him. Good-bye, darling."

The woman ends her call, and turns to her husband (age 55+), who is reading the business section of the newspaper on the couch opposite her.

"That was Susan," says the woman.

"Ummm… everybody doing OK?," we hear the man say from behind the open paper.

"Actually, no," replies his wife. "She and Tom and the kids won't be coming here for Thanksgiving dinner."

Her husband lowers the newspaper, and we see his face for the first time.

"But they always come here," he says. "That's how we do Thanksgiving."

He sets the newspaper down. "Is something wrong? Are the kids sick?"

"No one is sick," his wife replies. "Honey, they just want a different kind of Thanksgiving this year—a family Thanksgiving, one that's just about family."

Her husband looks perplexed. "How can you have a Thanksgiving about family if you aren't with your family? Linda, this isn't making any sense. Hand me the phone—I'll call Tom and straighten this out."

Instead of handing her husband the phone, Linda asks, "Do you remember what we talked about during dinner last Thanksgiving,"

"Now how would I remember that?" replies her husband "Do you?"

"Oh, yes," Linda replies. "We talked about what we always talk about when Tom is here: the business. That's what we talked about before dinner, during dinner and after dinner. The business."

"Well, we own a business, and Tom and I work it together. Why wouldn't we talk about it?" her husband says. He thinks a moment.

"Wait a minute," he finally says, "are you telling me that they don't want to come to dinner because they don't want to talk about the business on Thanksgiving?"

His wife nods.

"Well that's just about the craziest thing I've ever heard," says the husband. "Tom and I are at the plant 6 days a week, 10 hours a day. That business is who we are and what we do, and it's provided a pretty nice living for all of us. What does everybody think we'd be talking about if not the family business?"

His wife shakes her head.

"I wonder…" She says as we FADE OUT.


FADE IN later that day husband and wife seated on couch, drinking coffee. The husband is speaking.


"Let me get this clear," he says. "The kids don't want to come here for Thanksgiving dinner because they're afraid I'll do nothing but talk about the business, and that will spoil the holiday or something?"

"They're not afraid that the topic of the

business will dominate everything we talk about, John," says his wife. "They're certain it will. And to be honest, I agree with them. When we sit down at the table you're complaining about supply chain problems as soon as we serve the salad, employee turnover while you're slicing the turkey, and new government taxes and regulations while we're dishing up the pumpkin pie."

John sets his coffee down. "That's the way it is with a family business, honey. You know that. It's who we are."

Linda shakes her head. "I'm not with you on that one, not at all. The business is part of what we do, it's not who we are. Honey, I get what it means to own a family business... after 25 years, believe me, I understand. But for Susan and Tom, and especially for the grandkids, there is a bigger picture out there, one that doesn't include the business. I think that's what they want to talk about, too, not just the work."

John is pensive. "Do you think Tom and Susan feel like they can't talk to me about anything other than the business? I mean, I don't see that; I'm happy to talk about anything... sports, movies, fishing..."

Linda smiles, and places her hand on her husband's forearm. "Darling, I know that, and I appreciate your willingness to talk this through with me. But there's something a whole lot bigger than the quality of our dinner-table conversation going on here."

"And that would be...?" says her husband.

"The recognition that the business of the family is just as important as the family business," Linda answers.

"The business of the family," repeats John. "And by that you mean…"

"The things that make us unique as a family and as individuals, the stories we inherited from our parents, the life lessons and experiences we've shared that we should be passing on to our kids and grandkids. The things outside of the business that we would like to do as a family, all of us, together."

"And you think we should try to sandwich all of those conversations in between the turkey and the Bowl Games on Thanksgiving Day?"

Linda takes a sip of coffee. "John, this family doesn't have a Thanksgiving Day problem. We have an everyday problem. If something is not connected to the business, we don't talk about it much, and we do even less about it."

"But it won't always be like that," says her husband. "In 4 or 5 years I'll pull the plug, and we'll retire. There'll be plenty of time to visit with the kids and grandkids, and we can spend the next 20 years telling all of those stories you're talking about."

"And in the meantime,?" asks Linda. "We go 4 or 5 years without the kids and grandkids here for Thanksgiving or Christmas? We miss out on being a part of our grandchildrens' lives, all because we can't or don't want to do whatever it takes to just communicate with our own family in a more meaningful way? Honey, is that really what we want for ourselves and for them?"

John gazes into his coffee cup, then raises his head, and with a slight smile says: "Pumpkin pie with taxes? Really?"

"That and a little whipped cream makes for some pretty sad desert conversation," says Linda. She hands the phone to her husband. "Would you like to call Tom and Susan now?"

John stands up. "How about we drive over to their house and invite them to Thanksgiving dinner in person," he says.

FADE OUT.

# CHAPTER TEN

## Family Philanthropy

*We make a living by what we get, but we make a life by what we give.*

Winston Churchill

I t was the biggest box of chocolate you've ever seen," says Perry. "See's finest. Eight separate layers, each with, oh, at least thirty pieces of candy in each layer. Dark caramels, truffles drizzled with raspberry sauce, chocolate with little almond slivers, and those little bon-bon things. When I lugged it into the meeting room and plopped it on the table, twenty-five pairs of eyes lit up like it was Christmas. I didn't know attorneys and financial planners could drool like that!"

The setting was a Heritage Institute presentation for advisors to affluent families. Perry had just purchased the biggest, heaviest, and the greatest gift (or, depending on your viewpoint, the worst temptation) they could find in Chicago. (When he carted the massive box up to the See's candy counter and told the clerk that the twelve pound giant was for a business meeting, not for him personally, the *I've seen-it-all-before* salesperson just said, "Sure, fella... whatever you say.")

At the presentation, Perry pulled the top off the large box, and slid it to the nearest person seated at the U-shaped conference table. "We want you to have as much of this candy as you'd like," he said. "But, you need to eat whatever you take right now, and we need to eat it up before we leave today." The combination of the words great chocolate, free, and all-you-can-eat didn't fall on deaf ears. As the massive container was pushed from person to person along the table, most took at least two pieces. For the next five minutes the only sounds in the room were the rustle of candy wrappers, an occasional "That is so good," and a few, "Did you try the ones with the pecans?"

When the box reached the far end of the room, and everyone had had their first shot at the candy, Rod picked up the box and carried it back to the head of the line. "Okay, time for the second course," he said. And around the room the box went again. Most folks took just one piece this time, a few sighed, and waved it past (maybe with the just the slightest regret). The second trip around the room took only a couple of minutes. Once again, Rod carried it back to the other side, and urged folks to take their fill. Only a couple of hardy souls reached for thirds. The room grew quieter as confectioners' sugar and cocoa powder began to work their sleepy magic on people who only twenty minutes earlier had greeted the arrival of the chocolate feast with loud approval.

"Well," said Perry when the box came to a complete stop, "we've only eaten the two top tiers. There are still six layers left. How about we send it around just one more time? Anybody up for that?" There were no takers. As good as the chocolate was, as infrequently as they may have had opportunities to indulge all they wanted, sometimes, enough is enough.

Just then, the door to the conference room opened, and a member of the hotel staff quietly entered. Her job was to check and refill the coffee and other refreshments on the table at the back of the room. Perry called out to her, "Excuse me, miss—would you mind coming up here for a minute?"

She hesitated. Standing in front of a room filled with hotel guests at the conferences where she worked wasn't something she did. She approached Perry, and he asked her to turn with him to face the people at the table.

"Do you mind if I ask your name?" he said.

"I'm Magdalena," she replied, quietly, unsure about what it was they wanted to speak to her.

"Well, Magdalena," continued Perry, "I just wanted to take a minute and thank you for all you've done for us the past couple of days. You've kept the break table stocked, you've answered questions about the area for our folks, and you've been really pleasant and helpful. We appreciate that."

The twenty-five advisors gave her a round of applause. "Now," said Perry, "we'd also like you to have something, our way of saying thanks. Do you have children?"

"Yes," said Magdalena. "I have four, ages three to ten."

"Well, they're going to love this," replied Perry as he handed her the box of candy. "We had a few pieces ourselves, but I think there will be plenty for your children."

She took the (now just) ten pound box, her face beaming in a wide smile. The attorneys and financial advisors broke into applause again. Each one of them felt as if they had personally given her the candy.

Magdalena nodded to the group, thanked Perry and Rod, and left the room.

When she had gone, Perry turned to the group and asked, "So, which felt better? Seeing that wonderful candy come in here this morning and getting to eat every bit of it you wanted or watching Magdalena's face light up when we gave it to her to share with her kids? That's what an active program of philanthropy can do for the families you work with."

Philanthropy is a remarkable tool. It doesn't just cause people to feel good about themselves. It can strengthen, unite, and focus the energy of the family in ways nothing else can. For that reason, it is an important part of heritage design.

,,,

A century ago, Andrew Carnegie and John D. Rockefeller spent fortunes establishing libraries, museums, universities and concert halls. Early philanthropists funded important medical research into disease prevention and cure, and even underwrote expeditions into the last uncharted wilderness areas on the globe. There was a strong religious component to much of this early philanthropy. The fantastic wealth of the great American tycoons often weighed heavy on their consciences.

Sheer wealth, however, is not one of the criteria for giving. When you combine American charitable giving with that other uniquely American tradition, volunteerism, you see that the instinct to share resources, including personal time, cuts across all economic boundaries. (It is interesting to note the point at which wealthy Americans become involved in giving. According to J.P. Morgan Private Bank, Americans seem to start giving "serious" chunks of their money away once they are worth around twenty million dollars, whereas in other countries the threshold is around one hundred million dollars.)

Earlier we cited a statistic from the Boston College of Social Welfare, which estimated that over the next four decades some forty-one trillion dollars will be transferred from one generation to the next. Paul Schervish, one of the authors of the study, estimates that as much as six trillion dollars of that transfer might be devoted to philanthropic purposes. Schervish also says there has been a fundamental shift in the motivation for giving:

According to Schervish, the rich used to give money only when they were scolded into it. Now they are increasingly giving out of a sense of doing something they want to do, that meets the needs of others, that they can do better than commercial interests, government or existing philanthropy. They can express gratitude for their wealth, and their identification with others less fortunate, and that makes them happy.

One of the things that "makes them happy" is the emerging consensus among advisors, counselors, non-profit organizations and affluent families themselves, that a family-based program of philanthropy is the most powerful tool there is for encouraging personal responsibility, accountability and family unity. Heritage advisors often hear parents say that their children never had a healthy appreciation of the power of money to do genuine good until they began to get involved in philanthropic activities.

What is so special about philanthropy? For one thing, it works on so many levels of human consciousness: for the nineteenth century robber barons, charitable giving soothed religious guilt for having so much in a world where so many had so little. For others, supporting charity has meant getting plenty of ego strokes. Think Beverly Hills charity balls, paparazzi, and enough Botox to petrify a national forest.

Beyond guilt and ego, however, lie the deeper emotions, emotions that philanthropy also enhances. First, is the idea of personal significance. In his book, *The Denial of Death*, Pulitzer-Prize-winning author Ernest Becker said, *"This is mankind's age-old dilemma; in death what man fears isn't extinction, but extinction without significance. Man wants to know that somehow his life has counted, that he's left a trace that has meaning. Its effects must remain alive in eternity in some way."*

Philanthropy does just that. Through it, people can experience the deeper significance about which Becker wrote. For families, that experience becomes exponential in its power and possibility. The trace you leave with your children through philanthropy can accumulate in their lives, and spread and multiply as it is passed to their children, and to their children's children, for generations. The disease of affluenza, which is caused by receiving money without meaning, can be cured by philanthropy, which makes money meaningful.

> , , ,

## Transformational Philanthropy

Rod Zeeb often asks his clients: "Do you want your children/grandchildren to be donors or philanthropists?" He has never had to define the difference—they know intuitively. The answer is always the same: philanthropists.

Webster's defines "philanthropist" as "one who makes an active effort to promote human welfare." A "donor" is defined as "one that gives, donates, or presents something." One of Rod's clients described the difference between a donor and a philanthropist this way: a philanthropist gives from their soul; a donor gives from their wallet. Another person said: "a donor goes to the charity's auction to buy something (that they want or need!) at a discount, and then seeks recognition as a donor for doing so. A philanthropist is the one who donates those items or spends their precious time obtaining the items in order to fulfill the mission of the organization."

In our experience, a donor becomes a philanthropist through the act of giving a gift that is nothing short of transformational. It is the experience of joy and meaningful accomplishment that comes from fulfilling their passions that inspires them to commit more of their time and money to organizations that allow them to fulfill their passions.

"Transformational philanthropy" is a relatively new term. Here is an easy way to understand the concept: imagine a gift that has as profound an impact on the donor who makes it (and often their family) as it does on the organization receiving the gift. That is the essence of transformational philanthropy.

One of the most interesting things about the transformations that take place with this kind of gift is that there is no relationship between the size of the gift and the degree of transformation it can bring about. The transformation occurs not as a function of the size of the gift, but instead as a reflection of the passion behind the gift.

, , ,

Philanthropists *overwhelmingly* desire to pass their philanthropic passion on to their children. So, how does a family go about identifying and launching their philanthropic pursuits? These are key questions. First, we should be clear that the kind of philanthropy we're talking about is not necessarily the tried and true family foundation. What we really focus on in heritage design is helping the family match its deeply held values with a concrete vision for the future in which all family members play an important role. All too often, traditional family foundations exist only in legal documents, coming to the surface for "action" once or twice a year, usually around April fifteenth.

Our position is that affluenza can be avoided by teaching children a healthy, honest relationship with wealth. That lesson is often learned best through philanthropy. The idea will never take hold if they are simply handed copies of the family foundation annual report each January. This kind of education needs to be hands-on.

Your children will benefit from the actual experience of researching non-profit organizations. Some families get this started by giving each of their children a small budget (say $1,000 per year—the amount really isn't important.) Before a child can make a donation to a cause, they must research it. Where does the organization get its funding? For what does it spend the money? What percentage of its budget goes for administrative costs, and what percent actually makes it "on the ground"?

In his classic book *Innovation and Entrepreneurship*, management expert Peter Drucker said *"Don't over fund projects—you'll ruin them."* He knew that the most successful businesses and the best ideas are born out of scarcity. Great concepts more often come from struggling entrepreneurs in garage workshops than from teams of highly paid consultants sipping lattes around polished conference tables.

The same principle can be applied to children: "Don't over fund children—you'll ruin them. It will impair their character and destroy their motivation to succeed." When children study the plight of people in need, and they understand that they have the wherewithal to do something about it, it is a powerful experience. That is especially true of children who have never experienced scarcity in any respect. With knowledge about the needs of others, children can experience scarcity from the vantage point of the helping hand in the field. As one advisor put it, "Instead of merely sailing on a sea of riches, children can experience an ocean of needs."

When children are given a challenge and the means to do something about it, a whole host of positive decision-making skills will be put to use and honed. They may come to the conclusion (on their own!) that money alone can never solve the ills of the world, an observation which will enhance their maturity and put their own relationship with money in sharper focus. They can study and choose between dozens of charitable organizations and countless worthy causes "competing" for their attention and their money, which will sharpen their discernment skills and help them understand that real life is filled with hard choices.

, , ,

One parent told us a story about his thirteen-year-old daughter, Janine. She and her two brothers had each been given $1,500 and charged with researching at least three charities of their choice before reporting back to the family. Then they could send their checks.

A week before the meeting date, Janine had not started her research. Boys, cheerleading practice, her cell phone and the neighborhood mall took up most of her spare time. Finally, her parents had to give her an ultimatum: choose some groups to study, and prepare your report, or your four favorite activities would be out the door for a while.

"Yeah, well, fine," Janine pouted. "I guess I'll study about starving kids in Africa or something."

The next Saturday, the family sat at the kitchen table to listen to the charitable giving plans. Janine's sixteen-year-old brother Peter reported that he had just about been ready to select an organization that bought used farm equipment in the US and shipped it to Mexico as his preferred choice when, as he put it, he "figured out" how to read their financial disclosure report.

"Do you know that they spend 78¢ of every dollar that people give them for salaries and administrative costs?' he said. "That is so bogus! Only 22¢ of every dollar they get actually goes to buy farm equipment... if I gave them my $1,500, only about $300 would even go to the people who need it." So, he had found a smaller organization that relied on volunteers to deliver the equipment to rural Mexican farms.

"And they only need 18¢ of every donated dollar to do exactly the same thing. That is way cool."

Anthony, the eleven-year-old, had visited three animal shelters in neighboring communities. They all seemed to do a pretty good job, and they were all staffed by volunteers, but the one that caught his attention was about to do a direct mail campaign about spaying and neutering pets to every household in the county. "They had a sign on a bulletin board asking if people could help with the cost of printing and postage," he said. "They needed $5,000 in all, so I decided to give them half of my $1,500 and then to split the rest between the other two shelters. They both seemed like they had too many pets and not enough cages."

Now, it was Janine's turn. Her parents weren't sure what to expect; she hadn't exactly been a fireball of enthusiasm when it came to doing her research. So they were surprised by what they heard.

"I have decided to give my money to a foundation that trains teachers in equatorial Africa," Janine announced.

"But, honey," said her mother, "we thought you were researching organizations that deliver food to hungry people? How did you go from that to helping to fund teacher training... you've told us that teachers are the lowest life forms on the planet!"

"Well," said Janine, "they still are, at least my teachers in America are. But when I started to study world hunger I discovered that about one thousand children die every hour of every day from starvation and preventable diseases, like measles and stuff.

And I really wanted to just give my money to one of the groups that buy lots of food and send it to those places.

"But then I started to wonder, how come so many kids are dying from starvation in countries that have so much good farm land," she continued. "I mean, that doesn't make any sense. So I studied some more, and I talked to my geography teacher. After a while, I realized that the reason so many kids are dying isn't because they don't have enough food or clean water or medicine. It's that a lot of the leaders in those countries, and the people in power, are stealing so much from their own people, and fighting all the time, burning the farms and stuff like that. I just didn't think that sending over more food to those countries would do any good."

Janine's parents were quiet for a minute. This was their bracelet-jangling, gum-popping, iPod-blasting daughter? Their Janine was making these adult assessments, using this level of reasoning?

"I have to ask you," Janine's dad said at last. "How do you go from deciding not to give food to countries with corrupt governments, to deciding to give it to colleges that train teachers?"

"Oh, that's easy," Janine said. "I mean, if kids don't know anything, if they can't read and think for themselves, how will they ever change things? I guess if there are more teachers life will get better someday. I know it won't happen right away, but it's better than giving them some food that will just get stolen as soon as it gets there."

The next day, they family sat down together and wrote out checks for the organizations the children had researched. They also committed to doing the same thing the following year. For two parents, the power of philanthropy to bring a family together became very clear.

This is what can happen when parents give children a responsibility that matters, as opposed to another chore or a lecture. When children discover a passion on their own, when they learn they can make a difference, when they have the opportunity to come face to face with what poverty and scarcity really do to people, they can also begin to appreciate the proper role of money in their lives; as a tool to support the things that matter.

With heritage design, family is at the center of every long-term financial decision that is made. Family banks, family council investment clubs, grandchildren investment clubs, newsletters, family scholarship funds—these are all examples of values-oriented projects that put family before fortune, and which, through the process of diligently maintaining that perspective, end up strengthening them both.

The power of philanthropy to unite families in common cause is extraordinary. It does not require great wealth; there is no relationship between the amount of money the child is given to donate to a worthy cause and the lifelong impact that the project can have on them. Five dollars can deliver the same result as five thousand: a child who learns empathy, decision-making, over-the-horizon planning, problem solving—so many of the skills and attitudes necessary for a healthy (and happy) adult life.

If you have any doubts about the ways philanthropy can strengthen your own family, put it to this simple test… Buy a twelve pound box of chocolates, and call everybody to the table…

# CHAPTER ELEVEN

## Where are you today?

*Men go abroad to wonder at the heights of mountains, at the huge waves of the sea, at the long courses of the rivers, at the vast compass of the ocean, at the circular motions of the stars, and they pass by themselves without wondering.* St. Augustine

*People are usually more convinced by reasons they discovered themselves than by those found by others.* Blaise Pascal

Jedediah Smith was a young man in a hurry. And today, September 15, 1826, he was also in big trouble. The twenty-seven year old mountain man and explorer leaned over the edge of the rock-rim canyon and peered off into the distance. Behind him the sun was just beginning to peek over the jagged mountains. Directly ahead the barren landscape of the Mojave Desert stretched for miles to the western horizon, purple and blue in the clear morning light.

Smith's men, seventeen of the hardiest fur trappers and scouts in the territories, were stirring. The camp was coming to life. In a few minutes, the conversation that had begun around the campfire the night before would be picked up. Only today, Jedediah's men were going to want answers. Exactly where are we? Where are we going? How are you going to get us there?

Smith was no stranger to those kinds of questions. At the age of twenty two, he signed on with an expedition to travel to the Upper Missouri and trap beaver. A year later, he led another group deep into the central Rockies where he rediscovered the forgotten South Pass, the key to the settlement of Oregon and California. And tomorrow he would begin the last leg of the journey for which he will always be remembered: the first American to travel overland from the east, through the Great Basin, and then by foot through the brutal Mojave Desert (where it was so hot that he and his men had to bury themselves in sand during the day to cool down), to California and the Pacific Ocean.

By the time he was cut down by a Comanche war party near the Cimarron River in New Mexico at age thirty-three, Smith had traveled more extensively in unknown territory than any other single explorer in U.S. history. (A record not surpassed, by the way, until 39 year old Neil Armstrong stepped out onto the surface of the moon in 1969.)

Smith's life was made up of critical moments in which he had to ask himself (even when his men were not pressing the issue), "Where am I?" Imagine *walking* from Salt Lake to Los Angeles without bottled water, air conditioning, convenience stores, motels, roads, not even a map. (The tarantulas, fire ants, rattlesnakes, scorpions and other desert creatures along the way might inspire you to ask not only "Where am I?" but, "What the heck am I doing here?")

•••

"Where am I?" is a seminal question, whether it's asked on freshman philosophy exams, or, far less frequently, by the handful of men who will actually relent and stop at a gas station to ask for directions. It is a question that frames important issues in life (career, marriage, family, finances, faith), one that inspires the most important thinking, and the most crucial conversations, we will experience in our lives.

It is also the first question people ask when they get begin constructing their estate plans. The family-first perspective of heritage design expands this question to "Where am I, and where is my family, and where will they be in the years ahead?"

Most people are familiar with the "life planning" checklists that attorneys and financial planners provide for their clients. It's a good idea to have them and to keep them up to date (and easy to get to). They list the documents, policies, plans and instructions that make up the paper trail of estate planning.

You probably have completed at least some of these:

> Your Last Will & Testament
> Durable Power of Attorney
> Medical Power of Attorney
> Trust Documents
> Business Succession Plan
> Life Insurance Policies
> Deeds
> Beneficiary Designations

Your list may be shorter, or much longer, depending on your family, financial and business circumstances.

For most families, the documents that make up the traditional estate planning package are the proverbial *"last nail in the coffin."* They focus on endings, closure and finality. They mark the passage of a life, not the beginning of a legacy. Estate planning documents do the work of wrapping up old business (not the most pleasant way to phrase it, but accurate from the point of view of the professionals who are charged with distributing the dearly departed's assets) with an eye to dotting the *i*'s and crossing the *t*'s one last time.

Once the provisions of the will have been fulfilled, and the distribution of the assets has been accomplished, the thick manila file that represents the last vestige of the legal presence of the deceased person on earth can (and almost always will!) be sealed, boxed, filed and forgotten. The unfortunate truth for most people is that when the file snaps shut for the last time on the folder bearing their name, it also snaps closed on their legacy.

The idea of legacy lies at the heart of this book. Understanding what a legacy is, and how you can achieve a lasting legacy that will benefit your family for generations, is where our conversation is headed. The journey to the creation of a significant legacy begins the way all important journeys do, with the same question that Jedediah Smith's men confronted him with on that chilly September morning: "Where are we *right now?*"

, , ,

Heritage design asks questions that traditional planning does not ask because traditional planning does not take a stand on the future of your family—its only focus is on the distribution of your assets. To put it bluntly, traditional planning ends when you do. Planning enhanced by heritage design endures for generations.

Traditional planning is properly focused on transferring assets. The beans (your assets) are counted, divided and distributed. End of story. (Also the end, for the most part, of the involvement by the advisors who set up the plan.) Heritage design is about transition. The beans will still be counted and distributed, but that distribution will take place within the framework of a vision of a family plan in which the purpose of the assets is to strengthen multiple generations of your family in *all* of its interactions, both personal and business.

Like Jedediah Smith looking out across the vast Southwestern desert and envisioning his goal at the Pacific Ocean, heritage design looks into the future of your family and envisions the enduring role of your values as a living reservoir in their lives. That kind of planning does not come to a halt when you do. That's when it really begins.

We'd be the first to agree that when you ask the question, "Where am I today with my planning?" that it is a lot easier to get fast, snappy answers from the purely traditional planning side. Last will and testament? Well, it's either done or it's not. Family limited partnership-yes or no? Charitable Remainder trust? Check or no check.

Asking if your children can identify and articulate the values in your life that got you through the hard times, on the other hand, is a different ball game. But, which knowledge will better serve your children when one of them is facing a terrible crisis in his or her own life? Differentiating between codicils in a will? Or recalling that mom and dad faced some tough times themselves, and that they got through them with faith, determination, grit and hard work?

, , ,

Meet Jeff, a client who began the heritage design journey with his wife, four young adult children and seven grandchildren in the summer of 2010.

Jeff arrived at the office one afternoon, and accepted the offer of a cup of coffee. He'd scheduled the meeting without telling the assistant what it was about, so his advisor wasn't quite sure what to make of it when Jeff answered the advisor's question about how things were going with a wry grin and a slow back and forth shake of his head.

"The family's fine," he began, "the kids and the grandkids are all well, staying busy—even Katie is doing alright." Jeff's granddaughter had suffered permanent brain damage following a serious illness when she was 18 months old. Now 14, she would require around the clock care for the rest of her life.

"Angie and I are about to celebrate our 35$^{th}$ year of marriage, and business is about what you'd expect these days."

Jeff owned a manufacturing company that produced concrete barriers for roads and construction products. He built it from scratch, and now had about 100 employees making products that were shipped across the Pacific Northwest. Like most construction-related businesses, he had taken a big hit this past year as the economic roller-coaster continued to plunge and whirl.

He took a sip of coffee, set the cup down, rested one hand on each knee, and leaned forward. The advisor had known Jeff for years; this was his story-telling posture. The advisor didn't need to say a thing— Jeff wanted to talk.

"You know," he began, "Angie and I have told you how much this whole heritage design process has meant to us and the family. It's changed how we look at the big picture, and it's brought things out in our children that I never thought I'd live to see. We still have a lot of work to do, but the Family Council is starting to hum, and the grandkids will begin to participate in some of the family governance activities next fall. I guess I didn't know what to expect when we started this process, and I don't know for sure exactly where it's going to take us, but I have to tell you that just the simple act of creating a clear vision that the whole family understands and buys into, well, that all by itself was worth the ticket, it surely was."

"So, what have we got going today?" asked the advisor.

Jeff picked up his coffee cup, and pointed to the large office windows. "Things are pretty bleak out there, depending on your point of view, of course," he said. "I guess if you're in the repossessing business, maybe it's not such a bad time."

"My business is down 45% from this time last year, and I don't see an early recovery. People in my line of work, are hurting, and that's the truth. It was a cold winter, and I don't see a thaw coming anytime soon."

"You thinking of selling out?"

"Selling? Are you kidding?" He slapped his coffee cup on the side table and laughed. "Heck no, I'm not selling. I'm happier than I've ever been, more sure of things, too. That's sort of what I wanted to see you about."

In his two decades as an attorney, Jeff's advisor couldn't remember the last time a client burst into his office just to talk about how happy they were. That kind of action doesn't exactly fit the whole "reason-to-see-your-lawyer" theme. But the advisor could see that Jeff was energized by something that had really caught hold of him, and the advisor was becoming intrigued.

"Okay, I'll bite. Business is terrible, it looks like it's going to get worse before it gets better…"

"If it ever does," said Jeff.

"If it ever does," the advisor finished. "So, excuse me for being a little bewildered here, but just what is it about economic turmoil and negative cash flow that's made you so darn cheerful?"

Jeff leaned back in his chair, and smiled. "I'm disappointed in you. I thought for sure that you'd understand, what with all the work you do with families, and all the things you've figured out about what breaks families down, and what makes them strong. This should be right up your alley."

The expression on the advisor's face must have been a mix of clueless and sheepish; after all, lawyers, like doctors, are supposed to have an answer for everything. But, he didn't have a snappy reply, and so he just said, "Looks like you're going to have to educate me, Jeff. Why is a guy who might be facing the loss of everything he's worked for these past thirty years trying to convince his attorney that having a dump-truck load of manure dropped on his shiny new white shoes is suddenly a good thing?"

Jeff was quiet. Then, he raised his head and said, "Because... tough times saved my family when I was a kid, and tough times are bringing my family together now. I'm sorry for the hurting out there. I know folks are struggling. But, I can't tell you how many times I've said to myself that I wished my kids could experience some of the hard things that I experienced growing up. I am who I am because I had to fight and struggle every step of the way. My kids didn't. They never knew what it's like to go without. They had everything, they wanted for nothing."

Jeff and his advisor had gone through this conversation before. Early on in the heritage design process, during what is called Guided Discovery, Jeff said that the toughest times in his own life were actually the best times he had ever known. Tough times forged his character, honed his values and defined him as a person. Oh, he knew he was making it too easy on his own children, but, like many parents he went ahead and worked long and hard anyway so that his children would never have to sacrifice the way he did. A noble sentiment, his advisor had told him, but also a sure fire way to make sure that your children never had the opportunity to be tested themselves, or to learn for themselves just how much they could accomplish, even in the face of great adversity.

"So, how exactly are the difficulties that you are experiencing right now bringing your family closer?" asked the advisor.

Jeff stood and walked over to the credenza along the wall, where the advisor's assistant kept a bowl stocked with fresh fruit in the off chance that her boss might choose to eat a couple of grapes now and then instead of downing another handful of M&M's. (So far, the M&M's had nothing to fear from the competition!)

Jeff grabbed an apple, and returned to his chair.

"I'll tell you a story that I shared with my children at our Heritage Day last year," said Jeff. "When I was 10, my five brothers and sisters and I lived with mom and dad in a weathered old three-story clapboard house in Portland. Huge place, with a full basement and attic, and lots of trees to climb in.

"My dad never stuck with a job more than a few years, and this year he was selling life insurance. Door-to-door, I think. We didn't have much, that's for sure, and I don't think I ever wore anything but hand-me-down jeans and shoes until I was 18, but, heck, we never knew we were poor. None of the other kids in the neighborhood knew they were poor, either. We had nice enough homes, plenty to eat, and we could range all over kingdom come from morning till night in the summer, and our folks never had to worry about a thing. A guy couldn't call that poverty, could he?"

The advisor shook his head. Jeff had a keen understanding of the things that really mattered.

"So, anyway," he continued, "about the time school let out for the summer, my dad lost his job. He pounded the pavement for two weeks looking for anything he could find, but, times were tough— tougher than they are now. Nobody was hiring. He'd come home every night and soak his feet in an enamel basin, while he played guitar. Next day, he'd be at it again."

"After a couple of weeks, he and mom called a family meeting. They laid it on the line: we were broke, the rent was past due, and the phone was being shut off in the morning. My brother Greg wasn't even going to be able to play Little League because we couldn't buy his equipment. And, we couldn't borrow our way out since most everybody they knew were in similar circumstances."

"But my dad had a plan. Mom didn't share his excitement, but, in the darkest times, even a wild plan can seem like a comfort. And dad's plan was wild." Jeff absentmindedly bit into the apple. He chewed a minute, and then continued.

"Dad's cousin worked in the aircraft industry in Los Angeles, and business was booming; military orders and the early manned space program were keeping aerospace companies working around the clock. My dad knew a little about machine tool work, and his cousin said that he could walk in the door of any aircraft plant in Southern California and claim a great-paying job."

The advisor knew that Jeff had once lived in California, but he had never heard the details. He opened his desk drawer, and pulled out a small bag of M&M's.

"That was it," Jeff said, "we were moving to California. Us kids were up for the adventure, especially when my dad said he'd do his best to find a house for us near the beach. That cemented the deal— we were ready to go right then and there."

As hard as it was to think of Jeff being happy about his present condition, it was harder yet to imagine this gruff, middle-aged factory owner living the surfer life in Southern California. "So, you moved to the beach?" the advisor said. "What was so tough about that?"

"Now, don't get ahead of the story," said Jeff. "Yes, we moved to the beach, but that morning the other shoe hadn't dropped. And when it did, the whole moving plan suddenly didn't seem so bright."

"It seemed that when my dad said we were broke, he really meant it; we didn't have the money to rent a cargo van, buy gas and food for the trip, let alone rent a house when we got to California. If we really wanted to move, we were ALL going to have to go to work. That very day, in fact."

"How old were you again?"

"I was ten. My oldest brother was 15, my youngest sister was 6."

"And your parents expected you all to work, full-time? For how long?"

"Long enough to earn the money to move, and not a day longer," Jeff replied. "For a house that was usually filled with a lot of chatter and horseplay, it suddenly went real quiet around that big oak kitchen table. Real quiet."

"So, what did you do?"

"Mom told us to change into our oldest clothes. That wasn't hard, since that's about all we had. Then all 8 of us piled into the station wagon and headed south out of town and into farm country.

My dad had heard that Takashima Farms were hiring pickers, and paying by the day."

"What did you pick—berries?" asked the advisor.

"Strawberries and blackberries and pole beans mostly," said Jeff, "some blackcaps and marion berries, too. Every morning we would be assigned a row of berries, and given boxes or bags depending on what we were picking. When the boxes or bags were full we'd carry them up to the row boss to be checked, and they'd punch a little ticket that had our name on it. At the end of the day my mom would collect our tickets and take them to the pay boss, where we got cash on the spot."

"How long did you work?"

"Every day, seven days a week for seven weeks," said Jeff. "Mom would pry us out of bed before sunrise, we'd eat a bowl of corn meal mush with milk and sugar, and she'd pack venison or bologna sandwiches and apples. We could eat all the berries we wanted to, so dessert was free."

"And your little brothers and sisters worked, too?"

"All day long," said Jeff. "And every bit as hard as we worked. At lunch we'd sit by the river and cool our feet or chase crawdads from under the rocks. It was about as hard as anything I've done in my life."

He stood and walked over by the window. He pointed to the north and said, "Takashima Farms were just about 10 miles from where we sit. Malls and houses now—shame about that, it's such fertile land."

"You said that summer brought your family closer together, Jeff. Why was that?"

"Oh, lot of reasons," he said. "It wasn't just the working together part, though that was a big part of it. It was also that my folks expected us to be grown-up for a while, and they treated us with a new kind of respect and appreciation. We were tested, as individuals, and as a family. Man, when my dad would pull into the driveway at 6:00 or 7:00 PM, after nine or ten hours of picking, every part of my body was sore. We were tired, dirty, and covered head to toe in berry stains. The little ones would be asleep in the car, and we had to carry them to their beds. And when we went to bed, my folks still had to get ready for the next day, and plan for the move."

"But you know what? I don't remember anybody whining.

Not once. We were always scrapping before, like normal kids do, but not that summer. That summer we were a team, and we were all in the big game together. We knew what we had to do to get where we wanted to be, and we understood that there was no alternative. I know it's hard to understand, but even with the work and the sacrifice and the hardship, I didn't feel a sense of loss then, and I don't feel like I missed out on anything in my childhood when I look back today."

He returned to his chair, and the assistant brought him fresh coffee, whisking the M&M's away at the same time.

"When the picking season ended," Jeff continued, "we put in our last day and my folks bought us ice cream on the trip home. Then we all cleaned up, and gathered around the kitchen table. Mom pulled a shoebox out from a cupboard, and spilled its contents out on the table. There was nearly $4,000 dollars in that pile—more than most working professionals would have made for that seven-week period. Enough to pay our bills, buy a newer station wagon, rent a moving van, and rent a house close to the beach in California."

"I never saw my dad so proud of his family; and as for mom, she finally sat down and cried. I believe that was the first time since we all started picking that she had allowed herself a minute to think about it all. It was real quiet for a minute, I think we were all contemplating that great treasure, and thinking of all the work we had done together as a family to make our dream come true."

"I'll never forget the looks on my family's faces that day," said Jeff, "or the sweet strawberry smell rising up in the fields, or the feel of the warm brown dirt on our bare feet, or the smile on old man Takashima's face when he greeted us each morning."

"And now you want your family to experience the same kind of thing," the advisor said.

"They're going to have to," said Jeff. "I've got to lay off 25 people, and if my three adult children who work for me want to keep their jobs, they're going to have to work longer, harder and smarter than anybody else in the plant. I have to cut their salaries back, too, and there won't be a family vacation in Mexico or Hawaii this year, maybe not next year, either. I've robbed my own savings and retirement to keep things going, I put the beach condo up for sale, and I'm going on the road for a couple of weeks to help my sales staff."

"Hard times," the advisor said.

Jeff ran a hand through his curly hair. "The whole family is coming over to the house Saturday afternoon. That's when I'm going to break the news."

"How do you think it'll go?"

Jeff stood to go. "You know, when Angie and I finished Guided Discovery and our Heritage Statement, we were more nervous than a couple of long-tailed cats in a rocking chair factory. We couldn't wait to share what we had experienced. Our first Ongoing Family Council was last November—the markets had crashed and the rollercoaster was still headed way down. The committee reports weren't bundles of optimism, I can tell you that. But we shared the bad news happening around us together, and we talked about the future together, and we agreed that the best thing we could do was to move straight ahead with what we had set in motion. The kids are taking to the Family Governance idea in a big way, and no recession or depression is going to change that."

The advisor shook Jeff's hand. "It won't be like picking berries, you know. These are big changes you're about to drop in everybody's lap."

Jeff smiled. "You're right about that... in fact, I expect it's going to be a whole lot worse."

"So you came down here today to tell me that your family is about to go through some really tough times, and you couldn't be happier about it?"

"I came to thank you, and to tell you that this process has been a great gift to my family. I wish the country wasn't up against it, and that people weren't suffering. I truly do. But my family is prepared now, and I'll bet you dollars to donuts that when I lay things out for them this weekend, nobody is going to talk about the money first. They'll talk about what we can do as a family to ride this thing out, and how to come out stronger when it's over."

The advisor walked Jeff out of the building, and into the small parking lot. As he looked around, the advisor noticed something was missing.

178

"Where's your Lexus?" he asked.

Jeff pointed to a ten-year old pickup a few spaces down. It was clean, and looked well-maintained, but it was a long way from luxury.

"A picture's worth a thousand words," he said as he walked to the truck. "The kids will get the message."

Jeff opened the door, climbed in and started the engine. Then he backed up and pulled over to where the advisor was standing. He leaned across the bench seat and rolled the passenger window down.

"Besides," he said with a grin, "if we need to pick berries, I can get the whole bunch of 'em in the back—grandkids, too."

Then Jeff waved and was gone.

, , ,

Jeff knew exactly where he was on the day he visited with his advisor to talk about the huge changes that were coming down the pike for him and his family. He also knew, in part by virtue of the work that he and his family had done in heritage design, how they had arrived at the great crossroads. But the most important thing Jeff understood as he drove away in his pickup that afternoon was that no matter how rough and rocky the adventure he and his family were about to undertake (together!) might get, his children and grandchildren would come away from the experience stronger, more focused and capable as individuals, and more unified as a family. Jeff had no clue what his business or personal financial balance sheet would look like a year in the future. And that was worrisome, no doubt about it. But, he knew with absolute certainty where his family would stand twelve months down the road. That is what mattered most.

, , ,

There is a great scene in Mark Twain's American classic, *Tom Sawyer*. Tom and his best friend Huckleberry Finn are thought to have drowned in the muddy waters of the Mississippi. Their grieving friends and a few relatives gather in a small church for the funeral— along with the very much alive Tom and Huck. The boys have played along with the drowning idea for a couple of days, and now, they get

the extraordinary opportunity to attend their own funeral. Hiding
in the church choir loft, Tom and Huck listen as their brief lives are
eulogized. The boys can't help but break into loud sobs, and they are
discovered and punished. But what an image!

What would it be like to have a chance to fast-forward to your
own funeral, to listen in on all the conversations, and then to be able
to return to your current life?

*"Where are you now?"* questions transform into *"Where were you
when?"* stories at funerals. Where were you the day Jack announced
that he was getting married, the time he accidentally (maybe)
punched his boss in the nose, the time in college he stayed awake for
four days in an attempt to get in the record books? Remember how
he kept his employees on the payroll after the fire even though they
couldn't get back into production for three months? Mortgaged his
house, sold the plane, cashed in retirement plans...

Would many of the conversations at the service, reception or wake
after your funeral revolve around the "stuff" you accumulated in
life? (Well, except for the golf clubs and the airplane, perhaps.) That
would depend on the guest list, we suppose; but, just as in the case of
the two visions of the same funeral that you read about in our first
Video Break, when family and friends gather to recall the life of a
loved one, the talk goes deeper than the stuff. It goes to the heart of
a life lived fully through the telling of tales that illuminate not what
you owned, but what you valued.

When we ask "Where are you now?" we are actually looking
ahead to where you will be generations from now, in the hearts, the
minds and the daily lives of those who come after you. Would you
prefer that when your great-great-grandchildren gather for holidays
they offer a toast to the assets that you accumulated and passed on,
or, would like to see them raises their glasses in unison to you the
person, to the values by which you lived, and to the enduring legacy
of stories and life lessons from which the family continues to derive
inspiration?

*Where is your family today?*

A special assessment section

# Family Assessment

The following is a quick assessment to determine what areas are most important to you and your family and where you feel you currently are in each of these areas. This will help you to understand your priorities as it relates to the different aspects of WEALTH.

**Rate Order of Importance**
(5 = Very Important; 1 = Don't Care)

**Family Achievement Rating**
(5 = Mastered; 1 = Haven't Started)

| Rate Order of Importance | | Family Achievement Rating |
|---|---|---|
| 5 4 3 2 1 | Our family communicates well, and is effective at discussing sensitive topics. | 5 4 3 2 1 |
| 5 4 3 2 1 | I desire to minimize estate taxes, and have the planning in place to do so. | 5 4 3 2 1 |
| 5 4 3 2 1 | I have clear values that guide my purpose, and integrate them into my life and share them with the people who are important to me. | 5 4 3 2 1 |
| 5 4 3 2 1 | My family has a shared vision, and I have adequately prepared my heirs to effectively perpetuate that family vision and legacy for future generations. | 5 4 3 2 1 |
| 5 4 3 2 1 | Our family encourages open discussions and effective decision making. | 5 4 3 2 1 |
| 5 4 3 2 1 | I desire to ensure lifetime financial independence. | 5 4 3 2 1 |
| 5 4 3 2 1 | I would like my family to stay connected and unified, and have a structure in place to keep my children, grandchildren and great-grandchildren connected and unified. | 5 4 3 2 1 |
| 5 4 3 2 1 | My professional advisors work together as a true collaborative team, and not as individual advisors who share information. | 5 4 3 2 1 |
| 5 4 3 2 1 | I have prepared my heirs for the responsibility of both the financial and emotional aspects of their inheritance. | 5 4 3 2 1 |
| 5 4 3 2 1 | I desire to transfer to my heirs the family story, life lessons, vision and values along with my valuables and continue to do so for future generations. | 5 4 3 2 1 |
| | Are your heirs prepared to take on the responsibility of the family legacy and their inheritance – both the emotional and financial aspects? | Y / N |
| | Do you feel an obligation to prepare them for these responsibilities? | Y / N |

# CHAPTER TWELVE

## Defining Your Legacy

*In every conceivable manner, the family is the link to our past, and bridge to our future.* Alex Haley

*If you don't believe in ghosts, you've never been to a family reunion.* Anon

W e have guided clients through the development of their estate planning documents for over two decades. Wills and codicils. Living trusts, life insurance trusts and charitable trusts. Business succession agreements. Family limited partnerships and durable powers of attorney. We have prepared virtually every kind of traditional estate planning document, covering almost every conceivable contingency.

We have worked with clients who had concerns and questions about every imaginable financial possibility, from business transition structuring to asset liquidation plans to paying estate taxes, and on to the creation of trusts for children with special needs.

In fact, over the years, clients have asked us to create or modify estate documents to deal with almost any financial or business situation or family circumstance you can imagine.

Except one.

No one ever came into my office and said:

"Rod, I really appreciate the way you've done my will and my other estate planning documents. Man! That grantor retained annuity trust is something—and the way you crafted the reversionary interests clause, sheer beauty. Love the CRT structures, too. I know we're almost done, and ready for signatures. But you know, there's one other clause I want inserted. And this is really important to me to get down on paper—especially in a legally binding document.

You see, building my manufacturing business took up an awful lot of my time over the years; I didn't get that much time with my kids and grandkids. But, I want to make sure they grow up to be good people. Honest and decent. I want them to respect their spouses and their own kids, and I think they should do something for their communities, too. Plus, I want them to know the value and satisfaction of a good, hard day's work. What do you say? Could we squeeze those stipulations in somewhere between the asset distribution plan and the family limited partnership structure?"

, , ,

Rod smiles every time he tells that story. We both know that on the face of it, a request like that might sound downright silly. Even so, we have had some clients come pretty close. One man actually said, "Look, can't we structure my business succession plan somehow so that my son actually has to show up in person and do some work?"

Our answer:

*Estate planning isn't the place to do your parenting.*

It isn't the place to carve out your legacy, either. Estate planning has been—and always will be—a fixture of life in any society that permits the private ownership of property. There must always be formal mechanisms for the orderly transfer of property from one generation to the next.

What is worth considering, though, is that in the past several thousand years there have only been a few improvements made on the transfer process. From ancient Egypt to imperial China, from Victorian England to twenty-first century America, about the only thing that has changed is the terminology on the estate planning documents themselves. The intent of estate planning—to pass as many of the assets to the next generation as possible—and the mechanics by which it has been carried out through a lawful, organized process, have remained fairly static over millennia.

It is not as if every person who visited a lawyer in the past few centuries has been blind to the fact that their children would need more than money to lead fulfilling lives. But it is also fair to say that for most of history parents have assumed that what they left to their children in the way of material assets was the best, most important, useful—and practical—legacy they could possibly leave.

For much of human history, that was probably true. It has only been since the appearance of the modern welfare state in the past hundred years that most people were guaranteed, at minimum, an adequate amount of food, shelter and medical assistance to sustain life. Before the dawn of the twentieth century, there really wasn't much in the way of government assistance for the necessities of life. Personal responsibility was not a political catch-phrase—it was a fundamental requirement for survival. (We can cite any number of examples in history that show that for most people around the world, life was brutal, hard and short until quite recently. It was only about one hundred fifty years ago, for example, that over a million people died in the Irish potato famine.)

So, the fact that the essence, the impetus, and the overriding purpose of estate planning has historically been to keep the money in the family not only made sense, it made perfect sense. A parent's first responsibility to his or her children is ingrained as deeply as any other moral imperative: for the protection, the provision and the maintenance of life.

There was no compelling reason to change the basic building blocks of the estate planning process as long as the purpose of that process was so pure and unconditional. It was enough that the legacy a parent aspired to leave was bread on the table and a moat around the manor house. You don't need a trial attorney, for example, to make the argument that a pioneer family on the Pennsylvania frontier in 1763 would benefit more from a keg of dry powder and a brace of good muskets than from a family round table discussion about philanthropy.

That is the historical context within which the American tradition and practice of estate planning emerged. The purpose of planning was to sustain the basic life necessities of the heirs after the death of the parents. Period. And the legal system delivered. State by state, a complex framework of estate planning law and practice evolved to codify the process by which estates would be transferred from one generation to the next. In doing so, the concept of legacy was tied indelibly to the ownership of private property.

, , ,

The relationship between property and legacy has deep and highly visible roots. For thousands of years we have seen that when people of wealth and power wanted to be remembered, they usually set about to build something big, impressive and long-lasting the world would never forget. The legacies of Pharaohs were immortalized in pyramids and obelisks; that of the Renaissance Princes in marble palaces and commissioned art. These days, Hollywood producers vie for attention with their over-the-top monstrosity homes, and "everyday" millionaires give a few million to get their name inscribed on the dining hall at their local state university. From Sumerian King to American robber baron, the vehicle of choice for those wishing to leave a legacy has almost always had to do with property.

That perspective is changing. At the dawn of the twenty-first century, the cultural, economic and political landscape has changed to such an extent that the behemoth legal machine that powers the mechanisms of traditional estate planning is arguably out of step with the true hopes, aspirations and needs of clients. Perhaps especially when it comes to the idea of leaving a legacy.

For those who haven't checked lately, not many homes come with moats. Few children have to chop kindling and stoke fires to heat bath water, no armor-clad knights pillage around neighborhoods, and even the tabloid-crazed media would be hard pressed to find tens of thousands of people starving in the American suburbs. The historical notion of *survival of the fittest* (despite its brief incarnation on prime time TV) seems archaic and just a bit quaint in a world where food, shelter, medicine and education have become de facto cradle-to-grave entitlements.

The world has changed. In the past century the conditions of life for most people have improved dramatically and with blazing speed. Because of that, the ages-old social equation that said "*Legacy* equals *Property*" is simply no longer valid. It has not been true for some time. As proof, recall that 90% of all traditional estate plans, which hinge on the protection and transfer of property, will fail the inheritors. It is incomprehensible to think that the people who created the material legacies that eventually crashed down around their inheritor's heads actually wanted such financial collapse and family chaos to be their lasting legacies.

, , ,

Earlier in this book we cited a study that showed that the vast majority of adults believe that values, stories and life lessons are the most important inheritance they could receive from their parents or leave to their children. Despite that overwhelming sentiment, the survey also reported that fewer than one-third of those responding had actually done anything about translating those wishes into action. No conversations with parents or children, no family meetings, and no documents.

Old ways die hard; too many people are still focused on digging deeper moats around their castles, and filling their storehouses with grain as a means of providing a legacy for their children. The myth that the property you leave behind will be your ultimate legacy is a powerful one. And, like all good fairy-tales, it is a story told in virtually every nation and among most cultures.

When we talk about your true legacy, your significant legacy, and how heritage design helps you to formalize and communicate that legacy to your inheritors, we aren't suggesting that your property is "off the table" in that process, or that you're going to disclose the entirety of your estate to your children or other inheritors. Your material wealth is still important, but now it is important primarily in its role as a tool to support the transmission of your real wealth—the things that matter most to you because they *are* you.

Your personal legacy will be defined for generations by what you *valued*, not by the value of what you owned.

*Video Break*
The Estate Plan

**VIDEO: The Estate Plan**
*Location: Interior / Advisor's Office / Day*
We FADE IN as a man(age 40+) enters the
reception area of his financial advisor's
office. He is shown into the advisor's office,
where he settles into a comfortable chair in
front of her desk. The advisor welcomes him.
As they engage in a little light conversation
the advisor goes to the credenza and picks up
two thick notebooks. She slides them across
the desk towards her client.

"There it is," says the advisor. "The
fruits of our labors this past year. Your
complete Estate Plan, including everything
from your updated trust documents to your
business succession plan and recommended tax
strategies. Asset allocation, charitable
remainder trust, provisions for your special-
needs child, the works." The advisor is
clearly pleased with what she and her
collaborative team of professionals have been
able to accomplish on the clients' behalf.
The man picks up one of the notebooks.
"State of the art planning," he remarks as he
flips through it.
"The best," says the advisor. "We scoured
the new tax legislation with a laser beam to
make sure we get as many assets as possible
past the tax man and directly to your four
children as is legally possible. Your
attorney and CPA have crafted documents that
are about as close to foolproof as can be.
I'm sorry to say it, but if the proverbial
18-wheeler swerved across the highway and
sent you to your great reward today, your

estate would be positioned to transfer to your heirs with a minimum of fuss. Your children are lucky to have parents who have taken the time and expense to plan to make sure that they receive the things that matter most after you both are gone. "

"I wonder," says the man. From the expression on his face, the advisor knows that her client has something important on his mind.

"Are you concerned we may have overlooked something?" asks the advisor.

The man is quiet for a moment. "I'm afraid we may have overlooked everything," he finally says.

"Everything?" says the advisor. She indicates the two thick notebooks. "There are over 300 pages of detailed analysis in that package. 46 separate documents, each authorizing an action or series of actions designed to transition and protect everything you have worked for building your business on to your children. I'm not sure what we could have missed, but I'm all ears. What do you feel that we need to address in order to bring this plan to a place where you are comfortable implementing it right now?"

"Don't get me wrong, Lesli," says the man. "I have every confidence in the work that you and the rest of the team have done on our behalf. And I don't doubt that you have made sure that from a legal and financial standpoint that we are covered as well as anyone could be. We appreciate what you have done for us, especially the way you pulled the advising team together and on task.

It's just… we've been thinking, and the more my wife and I talk about what really matters to us, the more it becomes clear that there is a big piece missing from our planning."

The advisor leans back in her chair. "Would you like some coffee?" She asks.

We FADE OUT and then FADE BACK IN. The man has a cup of coffee on the desk in front of him. The advisor is holding a fresh yellow legal writing pad. "What are your concerns?" she asks.

"We were talking last night about my meeting with you today," says the man. "About how… I guess you'd say, how relieved we are to have our estate plan completed. No one wants to think about their life ending, but it is a comfort to know we've done everything we can to provide our children with the financial support they would need if we died unexpectedly."

"Here's what is troubling us, Lesli." He points to the two thick notebooks containing the estate plans: "Our plan provides for our children financially, but what about the things that matter even more to us than the money?"

The advisor says, "I'm not sure I follow. Are you asking if we can amend the trusts in some way to reflect some other requirements you want to put into place before your children can receive their inheritances?"

The man takes a sip of coffee. "No, not that. You see, last night my wife asked me one of those questions that makes you sit up and take notice, the kind that gets you thinking

about the really big questions in life.
She said, if our house was on fire, and the
children were outside and safe, and we only
had time to grab one or two things before
we had to get out ourselves, what would we
take?"

"That is a big question," says the advisor.

"But you see, it really wasn't difficult for
either of us," says the man. "We didn't think
about grabbing the laptop or the box in the
den that's packed with our financial records.
We both said, at virtually the same instant…
the family pictures, the scrapbooks in the
living room that are filled with photos and
old family letters. Things like that."

"I get that," says the advisor. "Those
are the things that are closest to us
emotionally. I think I'd do the same thing.
But, how does that impact your thinking about
your estate plan?"

"That's what we talked about way into the
late hours last night, and why I really
appreciate the coffee," says the man. "If I
may, let me tell you how our conversation
developed, and why I'm here today."

"Please," says the advisor as she sets down
her note pad.

"As we talked about what the most important
inheritance we could leave our children would
be, our conversation kept steering away
from the money. We talked about our family
history, all of our stories, the experiences
we have had ourselves and the stories that we
know about our own parents' and grandparents'
lives. We talked about the lessons we have
learned, the values that are important to us,

and about the people who made a difference to us as we grew up. My wife summed up what we were talking about with another great question: she said, if we could look 60 years into the future, a time when both of us were gone, and see a gathering of our family, what would we like to see going on? What would we like to hear them talking about, that kind of thing."

"What a wonderful idea," says the advisor. "I've never thought of the planning process within that kind of criteria. How did you answer?"

"I said that I'd want to see our children and grandchildren, great-grandchildren too, I suppose, living fulfilling, productive lives," says the man. "I'd want to see the family united, spending time together, maybe even taking on some kind of philanthropic projects as a family that everyone, even the children, could share together. And I'd want them to have a strong sense of where they came from, and what their ancestors were all about. Does that make sense?"

"It makes perfect sense," says the advisor. "I think we'd all like to envision our families that way in the future…"

"Including remaining financially strong," says the man, putting his hand atop one of the planning notebooks, "being good stewards of the assets that were left to them."

The advisor says, "And after that conversation with your wife, you are wondering…"

The man holds up one of the notebooks. "Where, exactly, inside all of this detailed

and elaborate planning for the future of our
money, is the planning for the future of our
family? They're not the same, are they. What
page do I turn to read about how we can go
about maintaining our family unity and our
prosperity generation after generation?"

The advisor smiles and shakes her head.
"We've known each other for 10 years," she
says. "And in all that time you have never
asked me a question that I couldn't answer
on the spot myself, or that I couldn't find
another professional who could answer pretty
quickly. The short answer, I suppose, is that
the page you are looking for isn't in there.
And I do agree that planning for the future
of your money and planning for the future
of your family aren't necessarily the same
thing."

"I didn't come here to sideswipe you, Lesli,
or to trash the planning you have helped
to create," says the man. "I know that the
financial inheritance side of the equation
is important, and it has to be crafted
carefully.

You've done that, and I'm grateful.

"But, correct me if I'm wrong, isn't it true
that all through history most families who
achieve financial success in one generation
usually see it all blow away by the third
generation? And isn't that true no matter
how completely and thoroughly the first
generation's financial planning was done?"

The advisor nods her head. "Once upon a
time it was just anecdotal evidence, old
sayings about the first generation making
it, the second generation enjoying it and

the third generation seeing the last of it
go down the drain. But it's not anecdotal
any longer. We have all kinds of studies
and advisor experience to back it up. 9 out
of 10 inheritance plans fail if you measure
performance out beyond a generation or two."

"Any reason we shouldn't?" asks the man.
"It's what my wife and I want for our
children, and theirs, and for generations to
come."

"And it's your sense that the team of
advisors who built all this," says the
advisor, pointing to the notebooks, "should
be able to provide you with some kind of
process or planning to keep your family from
becoming one of the 90% who fail?"

"I know, it sounds like a huge undertaking
on the face of it," says the man, "and I
understand that for the most part your
profession is concerned with the here and
now, not what will be happening 25 years from
now. But here's my question: if financial
advisors and attorneys and accountants know
the reasons why 90% of families fail when
it comes to keeping the family and its
assets together for multiple generations…"

"And we do," says the advisor.

"…then you must also know what the
successful 10% of families do differently,
the strategies and processes that they put
into place that help them to succeed where
everybody else fails " says the man. "So…
tell me what successful families do…"

The advisor smiles, and flips open one of the
notebooks.

"And make that the foundation for all of

your planning?"

"We've succeeded in building a plan that will pass what we own to our children," says the man. "Almost everyone who does some financial and estate planning accomplishes at least that much. But, if our planning is going to achieve what matters most to us, if it's going to equip our children and theirs with what they need to become part of the 10% of families who go on strong generation after generation, well, we've got some more work to do..."

"Maybe it would be a good idea for us to bring all of your advisors together to have this conversation," says the advisor. "I will tell them that you would like us to meet so that we can..." she hesitates.

"Tell them I want to talk to them about adding a third notebook to our planning," says the man. "And in that notebook I want to have a process lined out that can help my wife and I to pass not just what we own to our children, but also who we are. The things that matter. The things that will help our family to stay strong... for generations."

The advisor picks up her appointment book. As the camera rises up and away from her desk, she is saying "let's start by having that what matters conversation together with your wife..."

-end-

# CHAPTER THIRTEEN

## Giving & Receiving

*In our family, as far as we are concerned, we were born, and what happened before that is myth.* V.S Pritchett

For most of us, that statement rings true. We know a lot about our parents. A little about our grandparents, and next to nothing about our great-grandparents. Even if you have done some genealogical research on your family tree, for the most part, it is just that: names and dates on the branches of a tree. In the heritage design process, identifying the non-material gifts that came to us from our parents and understanding how those gifts have influenced our lives is an important undertaking.

A powerful experience sometimes occurs during Guided Discovery Process™ conversations with clients. If they spent much time with their grandmother as a youngster, for example, Perry might say, *"Describe your grandmother's kitchen."* ("Kitchen," the person may think? "What does my grandmother's kitchen have to do with planning for my family?")

But when they begin to talk, wonderful memories surface. They might recall the smell of home-baked bread, one freshly shaped loaf rising on grandmother's counter, the other, warm and crusty, ready to be pulled from the oven. Or they may talk about early morning conversations they shared around her plain Formica dining table. They may even recall the day that they realized that there was more to this woman than the quiet homebody their younger brothers and sisters knew; that this was in fact a woman who had lived a full life, with joys and heartaches that steeled her spirit, strengthened her faith, and infused her with an enormous reservoir of wisdom and grace.

Where then, in the sea of memories you have of your own grandmother, do visions of her bank account balances come into play? Could you possibly attach a monetary value to the time that you spent in her company? And if she were to appear to you right now, and tell you what it is she is most proud of about you, do you think it would have anything to do with your material wealth?

, , ,

In Frank Capra's classic film, *It's A Wonderful Life*, Jimmy Stewart's character is given a tremendous gift. At the edge of despair, exhausted, discouraged and all but defeated at every turn in his life, Stewart decides to take his own life. He plunges from a bridge into an icy stream, only to be pulled to safety by Clarence, a bumbling angel (second class). Stewart is distraught that, like everything else in his life, even his attempt to kill himself has failed, and he wishes he had never been born.

His wish is granted, and for the rest of the movie we follow Stewart on a journey which most of us (at one time or another in our own lives) have secretly longed to take. What would the world be like had we never been born? How would the lives of those we loved (except the children we never had, of course!) have been different had we not been there to grow up with them, to work and play with them, to stand beside them in their difficulties, to share in their joys? And what about our accomplishments? The businesses we built, the lives we changed, the people we employed, the causes we supported?

For the purpose of a great story, Jimmy Stewart got to see that had he never been born, the lives of just about everyone he knew, and nearly everyone else in his home town of Bedford Falls, would have suffered his absence enormously. Some lives would have been destroyed or lost, some businesses ruined, hearts broken, a town ravaged—all because one good man was not there to make a difference.

, , ,

The theme of *It's A Wonderful Life* has been a staple of literature through the ages, and for good reason. Unless people feel that their lives have some meaning, some worth and some lasting significance, there isn't much reason not to take the leap off the bridge into the dark water below. So kings have erected their monuments, and composers written their great symphonies.

Each of us, to the extent that we are able within our spheres of ability, endeavor to do or make or leave something behind from our lives that is significant. Frank Capra's film showed that even a common man could touch the world in ways that created a legacy of lasting value. That is why the movie touches people so deeply.

Sadly, none of us will have the full-blown dramatic opportunity that Jimmy Stewart's character enjoyed in the film. But each of us has known someone in our own lives who lit a candle and carried it through the darkness with every step they took. A grandparent or a youth pastor. A scout leader, a coach, a teacher, boss or mentor. Someone who personified values, exemplified good character, touched us, instructed us, and guided us.

These are people, from your own life or from history, who passed a living legacy directly to you. What has that legacy meant in your own life? Have you shared the importance of the values and lessons they taught you with your own children, grandchildren or other people around you? In our experience, people who do the exercises below consider them to be some of the most rewarding work they have ever done. They also say that sharing the outcomes of the exercises with their own families has helped to bring them closer together.

We hope that your experience will do the same.

*Exercises*

## Exercises

The three exercises below provide an insight into some of the ways that the heritage design process helps people to focus on the things that matter most. Don't try to do them all at one sitting, but do give each of them your serious focus in turn. When you've completed them, please be sure to share what you have written with your family.

We promise that you will get a response that will move you, and that will help to clarify why we tell the children and grandchildren of our clients that the most significant inheritance they will ever receive from you has absolutely nothing to do with money.

Please grab a pen and some paper, and reflect on the questions below:

## Person of Influence

To begin, think about a person who was a mentor or who had a significant influence in your life. Write that person's name down.

• What difference did they make in your life?
• How are you different now because of your interaction with that person?
• What did you learn from them?
• How did you learn it (for example, by their words, or at work with them)?
• How did your experiences with them affect your life? —Is that person still alive? —If so, have you thanked them? —If not, could you thank their relatives?
• Do your children know that story?
• What value would it be to them and to you if they knew the story?
• Did you tell them the lesson or did you tell them the story?
• And, if they haven't heard your story, would it be valuable for them to hear it?
• What benefit would it be to them to hear it now?
• Is the story written down? If not, when do you plan to write it?

, , ,

## That's All, Folks

For this exercise, please imagine that you have just stepped outside to collect your mail from the post-mounted mailbox across the street. Your mind is focused on things happening at the office, so as you walk into the street you don't notice the fully loaded eighteen-wheeler barreling down on you at sixty-five miles per hour.

Whack! And that's it. Curtains.

Tomorrow morning's *Daily* newspaper prints a one-paragraph obituary article (next to a display ad for all-season radial truck tires, of course). Don't feel slighted by the brevity of the story. That's about as much room as the average 1950s B-movie star will get! Anyway, there it is, just four short sentences, in plain black 11 point Times New Roman type. Your life. Beginning, middle and slightly embarrassing end.

Unless you are a member of British royalty (or someone who insists on getting in the last word in any conversation), you probably haven't gone to the trouble of writing your own epitaph. It's not on the top of the chore list for most folks. But, we're going to change that right now. In fact, we're going to give you an opportunity that very few people ever receive: the chance to have not just one, but two versions of your life story written…and while you are still around to enjoy it.

Please take a clean sheet of paper, a pencil with a good eraser, and a deep breath. First, print your name, and under it your date of birth. Next to your date of birth, write the date of your fatal encounter with the chrome grill of the massive truck (how about tomorrow's date?).

Next, sum up the highlights of your life in no more than four or five obituary style sentences. The who, what, where, when kinds of information you see in most obituaries. ("Phillip Jones was born in 1955 in St. Louis, Missouri, and graduated from high school in 1970. After a tour of duty in the US Navy, he attended UCLA, where he earned a BA in accounting. He started his own accounting firm in 1980, the same year he married Irene Martinez, with whom he had three children…" That kind of information.)

When you are done, share your work with a few people. Perhaps your spouse, your children or a couple of close friends. Ask them if the obituary sounds accurate. Then, ask them if that's what they would have written if they had been the newspaper reporter assigned to write about your life. If they are willing, ask them to actually write their version down. Don't give them hints or direction. Don't tell them you're reading a book about heritage design. Just ask them to write about you.

What they bring back to you might not look much like the formal obituary you wrote, or what the newspaper may actually write about you some day. Those who know you, and who love you, are much more likely to focus on the deeds of your life, not on the details. Their writing will be infused with memory and meaning. When they hand the obituary to you, don't be surprised if they're a bit self-conscious, even embarrassed.

When you read their version of your life story, you could see that it wasn't the company you built that they care to recount; it was that Christmas Eve you went without sleep so you could put everybody's bikes together. That's the kind of thing that they will always remember. It will not be your net worth that your children and grandchildren will tell their own children about when they share stories about you. It will be your human worth.

It is that human worth, built with values, lived through values, and evidenced as values in action, that will ultimately comprise your true obituary.

Heritage design helps people to identify that foundation, to shape that vision, and to share it with generations of their family. To get a feel for what that process is like, here is another opportunity to tell your life story to generations of your own family. This is a powerful experience, one that is worth keeping....

**Passing the Torch**
Write a letter to your great-great-grandchildren.
The purpose of this letter is to *"pass a torch"* to them. That torch is you. Think about what was meaningful in your life. What you did that was good, what you wish you could have changed.

What you hope they might discover to be true in their own lives, just as you did in yours. Please speak personally as you tell them things like:

"This is who I was, this is what I believed in, this is what I stood up for, this is what I did, this is the difference I hope I made, this is how I want to be remembered, this is what I really left my children, my grandchildren, and you."

We appreciate this will not be an easy task. Remember that few people get this kind of opportunity. Give it all you have. Don't rush. Don't feel constrained by the direction we have given... This is your opportunity to communicate the things that mean the most to you. One final thing: when you have finished this letter, place a copy alongside your other important papers, so that it will become part of the official documentation of your life. Include the instruction that it be distributed to your heirs, including the admonition that the letter be read aloud and passed on to each succeeding generation.

That letter can become the key to the most important legacy you will leave. That is a legacy defined not by what it was that you achieved, but by what it was that you believed.

You do not have to leave millions. Or build monuments.

*Sometimes, to leave a legacy, all it takes is a trip to the kitchen.*

# CHAPTER FOURTEEN

## Taking Action

*The way to get started is to quit talking and start doing.* Thomas Edison

S ome of our favorite memories exist only as "freeze-frame" images in our minds' eye. That is especially true of the paintings and drawings that illustrated the books we loved when we were children. The colors in those scenes seem brighter than those outside our offices windows today. That's probably the effect of a trick played on young brains which were not yet cluttered by politics, and work and the thousand distractions of everyday adult life. For us, some of the most magnificent and memorable images of childhood came courtesy of the great painter and illustrator, N.C. Wyeth, who single-handedly defined what classic adventure looked like for generations of American children.

In his illustrations for James Fenimore Cooper's *Last of the Mohicans*, clear-eyed frontiersmen battled brave Indian warriors in scenes splashed with mythical power.

He brought *Robin Hood* and his unerring archery alive with astonishing energy and bravado, and he sent shivers down our backs with his dark and menacing portraits of pirate captains in *Treasure Island*. Fantastic images, vibrant colors, adventure on the grandest scale. That was N.C. Wyeth.

He painted many more kinds of scenes, of course. But none of his famous landscapes or portraits held our attention or remained so fresh in our memories as his super-charged adventure illustrations. Until now.

, , ,

In 1941, Wyeth painted a simple country scene. It is set in the rolling foothills of the Adirondack Mountains, near dusk, on a clear autumn day. The central figure is an elderly man, dressed simply in a plaid shirt, canvas jacket and corduroy trousers. He is tall, with broad shoulders, a shock of white hair set above a handsome face bronzed by years spent outdoors. He is leaning over the top rail of a split-rail fence, his hands clasped around the bowl of a pipe. At his side, a black Labrador waits patiently for a command. Behind him, kindling smoke is beginning to drift above the cabin, where we can just make out the outlines of the man's wife through the curtain.

He is watching the car (a Woody station wagon) that pulled away from his cabin a moment earlier. It drove out and around the drive, turned left down the gravel hill, and is just passing below his vantage point. A man extends one hand out the driver's side, waving goodbye. From the rear passenger window, two young faces look up at Grandpa, their hands pressed against the windows.

Wyeth is a master of landscapes, so we expect to see the blended purples and greens and blues in the canopy of trees that cover the hills around the cabin. The softening afternoon light coming though the scattered clouds bathes the scene in a blue-gold halo, but that, too is not what captured our attention after all these years.

What is so remarkable about this painting is not the setting.

It is the expression on the old man's face. It's not what we would expect it to be. He is not smiling. He isn't returning his son's wave or giving a thumbs-up to his grandchildren.

In fact, his countenance is almost solemn. There is resolve in his eyes, a steely determination that has not been slowed by age. His head is erect, his gaze focused. Were he twenty years younger we would say that this was the face of an officer who was about to lead his troops into battle. Confidence without pride, conviction without arrogance, faith without reservation. This is a man who has thoughtfully and confidently made a decision of great consequence. Since we are watching his family drive away from his home, we can assume it is a decision about them.

It is true that we often see only what we set out to find when we look at paintings. As the years pass, however, we look with eyes that, having seen just about everything life can throw at us, don't tend to miss much. In this painting by N.C. Wyeth, we think we see just what the artist intended. His genius is his ability to transmit great meaning with just a few strokes of his brush. Complex effect from simple construction.

For us, this painting mirrors what we have seen in the faces of parents and grandparents during, and especially after they share a heritage design experience as a family. Facial expressions, of course, are tough to quantify, and all but impossible to define with scientific precision. (Just like a family.) Nonetheless, when families get together, work together and play together, their faces really do say it all.

Whatever family business may be conducted when they get together, and whatever projects are brainstormed for future consideration, there are some traditions that we encourage families to nurture and maintain. For example, the stories of grandparents, parents and others who have struggled, built, succeeded and just plain "hung in there" in the face of daunting odds should be given a place of honor in the proceedings. These oral histories (which many families decide to videotape) quickly become treasured heirlooms.

Heritage design encourages and promotes the telling of these family histories because they are more than stories. They are treasures, and in many ways the most valuable asset that your family owns in common. That is because the foundation of heritage design rests upon memory and meaning. The memories you keep of your parents, grandparents, the ancestors who came before them and other important people in your life are far more important than many of us realize. They are, in a very real sense, a kind of inherited emotional, intellectual and spiritual DNA. In turn, you will pass this "built-in" recipe for success or failure, happiness or despair, faith or hopelessness, to your own children and grandchildren.

Memory activates more than emotions. From a psychological viewpoint, memory is the actual fabric with which we weave our perceptions of ourselves and others. It is what we use to help determine how to instruct and guide those we love. Memory can be as selective and precise in recalling everything (what is it about those people who can answer all the questions on *Jeopardy*?), as it can be in stamping out conscious recollection of painful episodes in our lives we do not want to remember.

Out of memory springs meaning. The "why" of what you do with your life. Why your educational choices, your career direction, why the spouse you married, the home you built. And at the end of the day, memory will provide the assessment of for what your life stood. Did you beat the odds, and live a life of significance? Did your passage through life touch, inspire, raise up, or comfort others? Did you make lasting contributions to your community, as well as to those whom you employed or with whom you worked?

As we have seen, in the traditional estate planning process, questions like this are not raised. In traditional planning money is the focus. Its goal is to just pass the money, without concern for or consideration of the values, work ethic, faith and other important characteristics that created the memories and shaped the meaning that defines our lives.

Traditional planning does not look back to what it took to accumulate your money. It only looks ahead to the "iceberg tip" of taxes, fees and other obstacles that may stand in the way of getting more of your assets past the tax collector and to your inheritors.

*"If you want to know your future,"* said Winston Churchill, *"look backwards first."* Heritage design looks back before it looks forward.

It focuses on things that have deeper value to you and your family, rather than on the value of the things you have accumulated. As a result, the money becomes a tool again, instead of the focus for all you plan. Thus, the process becomes a multi-generational planning and training platform designed to pass what you really value along with what you own.

Heritage design has equal merit for those who do not have families. Through it, the single person or married people without children can discover and articulate the values they hold dear, and design a plan that can enhance the lives of others, or underwrite the efforts of the charitable causes in which they believe.

, , ,

In our individual practices, we have met with hundreds of families, from average income earners to billionaires. We know from experience that it is a bitter pill for successful people to swallow when their children or grandchildren fail to show the same kind of motivation, drive and ambition that helped the family attain everything it has. And we have seen that it is well nigh impossible for those same hard-driving achievers to understand (without some real soul-searching, that is) why the children they gave everything to can get mixed up in drugs, why they can't keep a job, finish school or hold their marriages together.

When any family crumbles from the weight of these problems, parents ask themselves a lot of questions. Why us? Why can't our children understand how good they have it? Why have I worked so hard all these years, only to see my family in turmoil, and my business at risk of just fading away for lack of a family member capable of taking charge when I retire?

If you share any of those concerns about your own family situation, by the way, rest assured that you are not alone: according to the 2012 survey of affluent Americans conducted by US Trust Bank, 78% of parents worry that their children's lives might be adversely affected by wealth. Affluenza is not only real, it's an epidemic.

, , ,

While it is true that no two families are exactly alike, most of them share remarkable similarities as it pertains to the way that their financial wealth affects relationships within the family. That fact, combined with the 90% inheritance failure rate, supports our contention that whether you value your money more than your family or your family more than your money, you're going to lose them both if you fail to address the Midas Curse head on.

We believe emphatically that most families are stronger than any divisions or disagreements they may have experienced in the past, or even any troubles that they may be going through today. Time and again we have seen families gather for a heritage design event and then watched as they discovered that the ties that bound them together were far more important than the disputes that had pulled them apart.

How do families get past the scars, recrimination and hard feelings that may have been years in the making? In part (and it is a BIG part), that journey begins as each individual discovers and acknowledges that their true wealth and worth as a family and as individuals has nothing whatsoever to do with material possessions. And when individual family members come to their own conclusions (for their own reasons) that the outcomes they want for themselves and their family is worth the work it will take to get there, answering the question "Can I really do this?" is a lot easier.

, , ,

Heritage design delivers what most people truly want to accomplish with their financial and estate planning: getting the family intact and healthy now, and maintaining that strength and unity in the future.

This is achieved by putting family before fortune, and by helping the family achieve and articulate a shared vision that will become the foundation for all of their planning. To get that planning organized and implemented with focus, energy and efficiency, each one of your advisors should understand that there are two immutable positions around which all of your planning will flow:

***1. Your children have already received their inheritance.***

Your money is to be regarded as a tool, not as a legacy. That tool is intended to bind the family together, and to promote family unity, individual achievement, and community involvement.

***2. The money is not to get in the way of your children's inheritance.***

To put it succinctly, the tail is not to wag the dog. No provision of your plan is to put fortune before family.

, , ,

Heritage design also facilitates higher levels of family communication in new and meaningful ways. It inoculates inheritors against affluenza, especially by virtue of the family's active support of and participation in philanthropic activities.

Through philanthropy, family members experience a reduction in the sense of separation from the world at large that many people experience. They come to view their money (no matter how small or large the size of the gifts that they can give) as a blessing that can benefit many people beyond their relatively small family unit, and they experience a greater sense of personal worth and self-esteem. Plus, the family that is involved in shared philanthropy projects creates a powerful forum for communication between generations and for practicing family democracy and power sharing. And, in an unanticipated side-benefit that we have seen in many families, as grandparents and parents watch their children manage increasing levels of responsibility with their philanthropic projects, it makes the task of "letting go" in other areas of the family financial picture much easier for the older generation.

, , ,

In one form or another, whether delivered formally by professional advisors, or informally by engaged parents and grandparents, aunts and uncles, cousins and teachers, pastors, coaches, Scout leaders and other influential people, the tenets of heritage design are what made it possible for 10% of families across the centuries to escape the Midas Curse.

It is our deepest hope that the 90% world of loss, failure and family chaos described throughout this book will be turned on its head—and in short order. Society has tolerated the Midas Curse for far too long. The social, financial, even political impact of family and wealth destruction left in the wake of historical inheritance planning failure is as unacceptable as it is incalculable.

The solution to making families stronger, more united and more prosperous is no longer a mystery. Heritage design works. It has worked for hundreds of years. Its basic methodologies and processes are widely available, easily accessed and many of them can be done without having to engage a professional. Your attorney knows it. So does your financial planner, your banker and your accountant. The question is, what are they doing about it relative to you and your planning?

, , ,

The last Video Break that we took in this book was titled *"The Estate Plan."* In that script we saw how one man sat down with his financial advisor and asked her to add heritage design to the financial and estate planning that she was doing for his family. If the multi-generational benefits of heritage design appeal to you and your hopes for your own family, why not bookmark *"The Estate Plan"* for your advisor(s) to read. We promise that by doing that one simple thing you will find yourself embarking on the greatest adventure you will ever take with your family...for your family.

# CHAPTER FIFTEEN

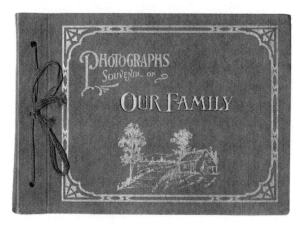

## Heritage Design & Your Family

What the chairman of Coca-Cola once said about his company is also true of families:

*"If every truck, warehouse and bottling plant we own burned to the ground tonight, and if every bottle and can of Coke on store shelves in the world was emptied in the fight to put out the fires, it would not diminish the value of our company by one cent. The value of our company lies in the hearts, minds and intentions of our employees, and in the good-will we have built with our customers over the years."*

You probably have one or more around the house. Up in the hall closet, under your bed, or stuffed into an attic trunk. Old binders, with cloth-covered cardboard covers, faint with the distinctive, musty aroma of age. You're careful when you lay them out on the kitchen table, and children are cautioned to turn the brittle pages slowly. Someday, you'll make copies. Someday, you'll scan them all into your computer, and add notes so that your grandchildren will know something about the faces that peer silently out at them across the decades. Someday.

To some people, the rag-tag assembly of subjects in the old photographs are little more than an embarrassing reminder of how unsophisticated their ancestors were. The grainy photos of simple, poorly dressed, weary-looking people only make them feel good about their own take-charge, speed-of-flight modern lives with all of its technological conveniences. They know the names of many of the people in the photos, but others are complete mysteries. Who is that woman holding Uncle Carl's hand? Is that Great-Aunt Edna as a child? Why is grandmother standing next to that store? Where was that farm picture taken? I didn't know there was a farm in our family. As for what that fellow we think is our great-granddad was named, or what he did with his life... unless there are hand-scribbled notes on the back of the picture, who knows? And let's not even get into what the old codger may have believed, or for what he fought, or what he sacrificed to provide for his family. How could we be expected to know that?

The truth is, if we don't see—and appreciate—that the old family album is a living history of the value and meaning of character, faith, endurance and hope every time we flip it open, we are missing one of our family's greatest legacies. The values by which your forbears and other important people in your life lived, are, without question, the most valuable and useful assets you possess. More important than real estate, investment portfolios, even cash. Because right there, in the unvarnished, honest faces of the generations who came before you, and the people who have influenced you, lie the keys to understanding everything you need to know to keep your family strong for generations.

Look again at the black and white photo of great-grandfather, the immigrant from the old country. He worked night and day to provide basic food and shelter to his family, sacrificing his own dreams so that one day his children would have a better life than he did. Photos of grandfather and grandmother, struggling to hang onto their farm during the Depression, sustained only by sweat and faith. Then mom and dad, with those silly grins, standing proudly in front of their first house.

Even without pictures, you can create a photo album in your mind, filled with living images of the teachers, coaches, pastors, Boy or Girl Scout leaders, parents of childhood friends, and other significant people from your own past. This is your true asset base. These mental images and old photographs represent the source of your greatest strength. They are also the most enduring gift you will ever receive, or ever pass on.

All of the investment advice from advisors and best selling business books, and all of the talking heads on TV money management shows, do not offer a fraction of the wisdom, the courage, the strength of character or the uncommonly good sense of the family, friends and other important people who have touched your life. The values in which they believed and by which they lived constitute the single most important resource you will ever have when planning for the future of your family.

The concepts of heritage design were born out of a conviction that real success as a family doesn't come just by planning for the *future* but also from recognizing and applying the lessons from the past. In the end, your own legacy will be defined by what you have valued, not by the value of what you have owned.

The process of successful multi-generational planning begins with the recognition of the values, ethics and traditions that are unique to you and your family. They may have come from many sources, but, if your planning is to succeed (which by our definition, means keeping your family healthy and strong for generations), it must reflect and embody those values. They will sustain and guide your family in the future, no matter the size of your estate. Common sense tells us that. Research studies verify it. But it has only been in the past few years that qualified advisors arrived on the scene who could help families make the leap from that common sense conclusion to a practical, proven, nuts and bolts planning process built on a foundation of your unique values.

, , ,

In the course of the heritage design process, families spend a great deal of time together working on a host of family issues that will help them become stronger and more unified right now and to stay that way for generations. Some of these conversations and family exercises may be done with the guidance of trained professionals at specially structured family meetings. Often times, the most powerful and enduring experiences that families share at such meetings come about as a result of activities as simple as having grandparents, parents, aunts and uncles and other family members sit down in front of the family and share their life stories. No theatrics, no props.

This can be a particularly impactful activity for affluent families, most of whom earned their money the old-fashioned way: through hard work and personal sacrifice. Studies show that seventy-five percent of all affluent people (defined as having a net worth over three million) made it themselves. No handouts, no winning lottery tickets, and no magic lamp with a genie inside. These are folks who have built businesses from scratch when scratch was just a couple hundred bucks, an old warehouse and a powerful idea. They've done every job in the building, from cleaning the toilet to painting the walls. They know what it's like to struggle and pray and dig deep in their own pockets to make Friday payrolls—most have gone more months without pay themselves than they care to remember. In the early days they held off competitors, crooked suppliers and government bureaucrats with nothing more than grit and determination and hope.

Still, it can be difficult for young adults or teenage children who have known nothing but the privileged life of upper middle class or wealthy America to really believe it when Mom and Dad sit down with the children around the dinner table and Mom starts talking about sewing patches on Dad's work jeans ("Dad wore jeans? Dad got his hands dirty?") Harder still to believe that Mom picked fruit in the fields for many summers so that she could stock the pantry when Dad's work slowed down each winter.

Tales of one room apartments, cars that should have been going to the junkyard but had to be kept alive for one more month, early business failures, banks refusing loans, partnerships that crumbled— and sacrifice after hardscrabble sacrifice—often bring the toughest businessmen to tears, and almost always leave their children with a new measure of respect for their parents.

, , ,

Here is a true story, one which illustrates how powerful and enduring the impact of the retreat can be for generations of a family.

Thirty members of the Danosovic family flew and drove from around the country to gather for a family meeting at a resort in the Sawtooth Mountains of Idaho. The father, Milos, is a successful manufacturer who, with his wife, had begun working with an advisor to integrate heritage design into their planning. His two brothers and their children, plus assorted grandchildren, also attended. Only his older sister was absent.

Also in attendance (for the first time) were Milos' eighty-six year old parents, who had immigrated to the United States from Hungary in 1957. Dave, the patriarch of the clan, was something of a legend (and also a bit of an enigma) to his family. He owned and still managed a thriving lumber mill in Georgia, where he regularly put in ten-hour days. He had loaned Milos the money for his own start up, and was somewhat infamous for the way he had forced Milos to keep to his loan repayment schedule even when times were tough for Milos and his own family. *"First you pay me,"* Dave was famous for saying, *"then we can talk about your family."*

His own grandchildren found Dave to be brusque, demanding, critical and deeply suspicious. He was also extremely sensitive to anyone getting physically close to him, and, so far as anyone knew, he had never shown any kind of physical affection to any human other than his wife. Milos had worked on his father for months to agree to come to the family meeting. He worked even harder to get the old man to agree to sit down and tell his story to the assembled family.

On the second day, right after lunch, Milos' extended family gathered in the great room of the rented lodge. Dave and his wife sat on plain wooden chairs in front of the fireplace, quiet, hands folded in their laps, deep in thought. Milos had never seen his father look so uncomfortable. It didn't help that Milos had been forced to threaten his teenage children with virtual banishment (no TV, internet, or iPhone…for the duration) if they did not attend.

They sat, glum and sullen as only teenagers can be, anxious to get this unpleasant bit of family baloney out of the way.

When everyone was settled, on chairs, sofas, even on the floor, Milos went to the back of the room and switched on the video camera. His father raised his head a moment, and glared, but didn't speak. "All-right, papa," Milos said quietly. "We're all here. Please... tell us your story."

The old man sat silently for a moment. Stiffly. People used to describe him as looking like a fire hydrant with a bad haircut. Those who had seen the octogenarian load stacks of pressure-treated 6" x 6" timbers in the back of customer's pick-ups faster than his twenty-year old employees just called him amazing.

Finally, Dave raised his head and looked out at the room filled with his offspring. "And, what is it you want to know then," he asked.

"Just tell us, papa," Milos replied. "Tell us how you came to America."

"Come on Grandpa," chimed in one of the teenagers, "tell us why you wear the same suit every single day." The children laughed. That was a family joke. Rich Granddad wore the same clothes, day in and day out. Every day. Every year. What was that all about?

The old man did not rise to the challenge. Instead, he looked at the teenager and asked, "What did you have for breakfast this morning?"

"Geez, I don't know," she said, "maybe some yogurt, some toast, oh, and a latte."

The other grandchildren giggled. But only for a moment. When Dave spoke next, the room grew quiet. It stayed quiet for the next two hours as he talked. No one left the room. No one so much as whispered. They just listened.

As he began to talk, Dave stood, removed his jacket, and rolled up one shirtsleeve. None of his grandchildren had ever seen him without a jacket. His own sons couldn't remember the last time they had seen him with short sleeves.

"897631," Dave said in a whisper. He turned his arm palm-up, and extended it so his family could see the crudely tattooed numbers etched into his arm. "That was my number—my name actually—in the camps.

Bergen-Belsen, Theresienstadt, and Auschwitz. 897631." He put his other hand on his wife's shoulder. She was deep in her own memories. A few tears rolled down her cheek.

Dave told his story in a simple, matter of fact manner. In 1943, he was a young Hungarian Jew, an entrepreneur with interests in several Budapest businesses. He was married, and father to a six-year-old girl. They were among the first Hungarians to be rounded up and packed into cattle cars by the Nazis. Their destination: Auschwitz.

Dave and his family were off-loaded in the vast field outside the main camp at dawn. It was freezing. His wife and daughter were separated from him, and quickly disappeared into the crush of thousands of Jews being processed for disposition to labor barracks, readied for transport to other camps, or, as in the case of many, directly to the gas chambers.

"I knew I would never see them again," Dave told his family. He looked at the granddaughter he had questioned about breakfast and said, "We had sour bread and weak soup for breakfast that day, on the train. The soup was served in the same tin containers we had used the night before as toilets. So, now I remember what I have for breakfast every day."

Dave described how he was made boss of a construction gang because he had some carpentry experience in Hungary. He told of the sleep deprivation, the meager rations, the indiscriminate murder by guards. "I worked," he said, "I kept my head down, I worked longer and harder and better than anyone on the crew. I kept my job. I let myself hope. I prayed. I waited."

After a year, he was transferred to another camp, and then to another. Skilled managers like him were in short supply. In the two years he spent in the camps he was beaten repeatedly, he lost three fingers to frostbite, and the only friend he made in the camps died of cholera. "I saw people shot because they bent down to pick up a discarded potato-peel," he said. "One night two SS guards drowned an old man in a fifty-gallon drum we had to use as a lavatory, simply for their amusement. He had done nothing to them. And so I waited, I worked, I hoped against hope, and I continued to pray."

Two hours had passed since Dave began his story. His wife had not moved or said a word. The grandchildren had slowly, almost without thinking, moved together in a tight circle. Several were holding hands. This is not what any of them had expected when they came to this family meeting.

Dave continued with his story. One morning in April 1945, he and the other prisoners awoke to find that the camp guards had fled during the night. The surviving prisoners gathered in the roll-call yard, shivering, hungry, uncertain what to do. The day passed and then another. They made do with what they could, scavenging for food and bits of clothing. They also buried hundreds of camp inmates whose bodies were scattered everywhere. They stayed put, mindful of the artillery shells bursting on battlefields nearby.

On the third day, a patrol of American soldiers arrived at the camp and told them they were liberated. "They had no food for us, or medicine, or even instructions about where to go," Dave told his family. "So, we began to walk. Thousands of us, ragged urchins, without money or weapons or food. We lived off the land. We stole chickens, and ate roots. When the war ended a few weeks later, we thought we were home free. For a minute, I thought I could finally rely on someone else for a bit, let someone else take care of me. Hah!"

His laugh startled the family. "The war was over, but we were not free. I wandered for six months, eating when I could, sleeping where I could. I prayed and hoped, but I no longer knew what it was I was praying for."

Finally, Dave said, he made his way to Vienna and to the vast refuge train station that had been set up by American and British forces. It was a major repatriation center for millions of Europeans who had been displaced by the war. Dave registered with the authorities and got a boarding pass for a train that would finally take him home.

"I pushed my way through the crowds. There were thousands like myself, all trying to get home. But home to what? For the first time since I was arrested and hauled off to the camps, I allowed myself the luxury of tears. I stood there on the platform with others going to my town, waiting for my train, in a crush of people as desperate and miserable as I was. I cried. I cried for my wife and my daughter, and I cried for my family and friends. I even cried for myself."

Dave's wife reached over and took both of his hands. She was sobbing now, her head buried on her breast. Dave's own eyes were moist, and tears flowed all around the room.

The old man took a deep breath and continued. "And then, well, it is almost beyond belief. The loudspeaker announced the arrival of my train. People swarmed onto the platform, everyone bumping against everyone else. It was madness. I was pushed backwards, and I stumbled over someone's suitcase. I scrambled to my feet, and I saw, and then I saw…"

Dave stopped. Tears were flowing freely down his face. He could not speak for a moment. Milos went up to him and hugged him. The grandkids held onto one another.

At last, Dave wiped his face with his one long sleeve, and said, "I saw my wife. Standing right there in front of me. My wife! And next to her, my little girl, not so little any more. Right there on the platform, waiting for the train to Linz. My wife and my daughter."

He could not go on. Deep sobs racked the old man's body. His sons had never seen such emotion in their father. They had heard bits and pieces of his story, but never the whole thing, not in this detail. Wives cried. Grandchildren cried. But everyone wanted to hear the rest of the story.

Dave's tears subsided, and he grew quiet. His wife picked up the story. "You see," she told her family, "when we were separated from my husband at Auschwitz, we were processed, and asked if we had any special skills. I was a fine seamstress, and I told them I had owned my own shop. A lie, yes, but, in such a time God forgives, no? I told them my daughter's small hands were expert at working with fine laces, and that she was highly trained, too. We were given jobs, and soon we were moved to another camp. It was not easy," she said, "but we survived. So many did not."

The room was quiet. Finally, Milos suggested they all take a break. The teenagers who had been forced to come to the meeting were the most reluctant to leave their grandfather's side—even for a minute. So much made sense to them now. They understood his gruffness, his impatience, his attitude about work and prayer.

When everyone returned from the break, Milos announced that the story wasn't quite over yet. "Mamma and Papa didn't exactly waltz here from Hungary in 1957," he said.

"Their adventure was only half over."

Now, Dave told the second half of his remarkable tale.

He and his family returned to Hungary, only to find his businesses had vanished, and his savings along with them. He started a small construction company with two friends, and the little company thrived in the post-war construction boom. They had three sons, including Milos, and they began to enjoy a prosperous life. Then in 1956, disaster: the Soviets invaded Hungary.

"In 1943, I was arrested for being a Jew," said Dave. "In 1956, I was arrested for being a capitalist!"

The new regime confiscated Dave's buildings and equipment and seized his bank accounts. Only hours before he was to surrender to police to face trial as an enemy of the people, Dave fled Hungary with his family. They made their way to Austria, and a year later, were helped out of the refugee camps and into the United States by a church in Georgia.

In America, Dave's credo of 'prayer, patience, work and hope' was put to the test once again. For the third time in his life, he applied himself, set goals, worked harder than anyone, and never looked back.

At least, not until this day.

Dave's story changed his family—profoundly and permanently. His children and his grandchildren's grandchildren will continue to tell the story, for generations. Four simple values—faith, hope, patience and work, will shine across the decades to illuminate the hearts of every member of Dave's family.

The values that carried him through some of history's darkest days won't simply be recalled in the isolated context of Dave's experience, either. Since their family meeting, those values have been enshrined by the family as the foundation for all of the business and philanthropy they will do together. They even had an artist design a family crest emblazoned with Dave's values. It was used to make a family seal that is used to stamp every family council document they produce.

Dave's story is remarkable, and it is unique, but the truth is that every family has its own remarkable stories of trials and triumphs. Sadly, most families (extended or otherwise) do not hold family meetings. Most families get together only at weddings and funerals. So, the stories seldom get told, and the life-changing, unvarnished lessons that they offer do not make it to the very people who need to hear them the most.

, , ,

We leave you with this final thought exercise. Find a quiet place where you will be undisturbed. Then, imagine that you are seated at one end of a very long oak table in a great, vaulted hall. To your left, extending so far out into the distance that you can only make out the dim outlines of faces, sit your great-great-great-great grandparents. Next to them are their children, and then theirs, all of your ancestor up to and including your own parents, who sit on your immediate left.

These are the men and women who fought the wars that shaped continents, who put the muscle and the brain into the Industrial Revolution, and who died at places like Little Round Top and Flanders Field and Iwo Jima. They tamed the Great Plains and built cities and schools and factories. They raised families under impossible conditions, and through the best and the worst that history wrought, *persevered* through the power of faith and the daily application of values that defined every aspect of their lives.

This is your family. Gathered right here beside you, alive, brimming with stories of sacrifice and success, love and loss. A family woven together by a thread of values, stories and experiences that intertwine across centuries, and that will survive your passing, and your children's, for generations to come. Hundreds of men and women, some in simple wool jackets, some in frontier calico, others in colonial lace. The heroes, the sinners, the providers, the builders, the scoundrels and the solid, common working folk who are your ancestors. The kinds of ancestors we all share.

Now, turn your gaze away from those who came before you, and look to your right.

As you peer down the length of the table to a point far off in the distance, a place where a few rays of sunshine are just breaking through a wisp of clouds, imagine this: on your immediate right sit your children.

Next to them sit their children, and then your great-grandchildren, great-great grandchildren, and generations of their grandchildren. Dozens of generations yet to be born.

Unlike the ancestors to your left who lived their lives, each in different measure, and who now talk and laugh of times gone by, the heirs seated to your right are quiet. Each sits expectantly. Hope and anticipation fill their eyes.

Each holds an empty glass in his or her hand. Your task is to fill that glass to the brim. Fill it with memory and meaning, with values that encourage, uplift and motivate. Fill it with faith, honor, respect, and love. Fill it with your story.

When you leave a legacy that is built upon that kind of foundation your descendants will not simply know your story. They will remember your name, what you stood for and believed in. They will honor your memory.

As you reflect upon the gifts that each generation before you passed to its successor, and as you use those gifts to make your own contributions to your family legacy, you do your family—past, present and future— a great service.

We promise this: as your family shapes its own heritage vision, melding what matters in your lives today with the unique values, experiences, life lessons, hopes and dreams represented at that long, long table....miracles *can* occur.

*We've seen it happen many times.*
*It can happen for your family, too.*

, , ,

## Some Closing Questions

The Midas Curse is all too real. It impacts 9 out of 10 families, and it is no respecter of income, status or wealth. Addressing the Midas Curse is important for all families, no matter their material wealth, and it is especially critical for the affluent, who, as centuries of history shows, have suffered the loss of vast amounts wealth in addition to experiencing chaos within their families.

It is in the spirit of that reality that we leave you with two important questions:

*Are your children (and/or grandchildren) prepared for the inheritances they will receive?*

*And, do you believe it is your responsibility to prepare them?*

If you are among the handful who have prepared their children/grandchildren for both the emotional as well as the financial inheritances they will someday receive, congratulations! Your accomplishment in the face of such daunting odds is something of which to be proud. We hope that you will share your story with everyone.

If, on the other hand, you answered "no" to the first question above, and "yes" to the second question, you now have the opportunity to embark upon the greatest adventure that your family will ever share together. (With *together* being the key word here.)

We do not pretend that the journey will be without its challenges. Nothing worthwhile ever is. What we can assure you is that from the outset, no matter how you begin your heritage design journey, by yourself or under the guidance of a trained professional advisor, you will begin to see changes in your family almost immediately.

The real changes that your commitment to heritage design will bring about in your family, of course, will occur on a multi-generational basis. In effect, you and your family will plant the heritage design tree today so that generations of your family to

227

follow may enjoy the shade that it produces.

For those who are ready to embark, a good place to begin is by sharing the exercises you did in this book with family members. Heritage design is founded upon solid communication within the family—and the exercises are a great place to begin.

We also suggest that you have a heritage design conversation with your financial advisor, accountant, attorney, etc. Let them know that you are shaping a new vision for your family's present and its future. Share "The Estate Plan" video script on page 191with them, too, and ask them how they can help you and your family achieve what matters most to you, starting right now.

Finally, if you wish more detailed information, or introductions to advisors who are trained to provide heritage design services, please feel free to contact us directly, or have your advisor contact us at:

info@gemisu.com

# APPENDIX

# About the Authors

## Perry L. Cochell

Perry began his career with the Boy Scouts of America (BSA) in 1994 in the position of Associate Regional Director/Senior Endowment Counsel, Western Region. In this capacity, Perry has supported council professionals and volunteers in the development and implementation of endowment programs. He has provided technical expertise in all areas of tax for current and deferred gifts to councils.

In 2006, Perry was appointed to the position of National Senior Endowment Counsel, National BSA Foundation, where he worked with the foundation director, related national and regional staff, and the Foundation Advisory Committee to secure major gifts to the BSA, BSA-Foundation and/or Local Councils.

Perry L. Cochell was appointed to the position of Director, Office of Philanthropy, November of 2009. He works closely with the Assistant Chief Scout Executive of the Development Office, the Chief Scout Executive and related National Board members to secure Legacy Gifts defined as outright gifts amounting to $10 million or more.

Perry earned his Doctorate of Jurisprudence from Willamette University, College of Law in Salem, Oregon. He completed his graduate studies at Brigham Young University in Provo, and earned a Bachelor of Arts degree from Arizona State University in Tempe, AZ. Perry has practiced in the areas of Business, Benefits, and Trusts and Estates Tax Law.

He is a Member of the American Bar Association (ABA) and is a committee member of the ABA's section on Taxation and Property, Probate and Trust Law. He is a committee member of the Emotional and Psychological Issues in Estate Planning of the Real Property, Probate and Trust Law Section of the ABA. Perry also has served on various ABA Task Forces for Charitable Giving. As a member of the Idaho State Bar Association (ISB), Perry has also been the chairman of the Legislative Committee of the (ISB) Tax Section as well as past chairman of the Current Affairs Committee of the ISB Tax Section.

Perry is co-founder and Certified Wealth Consultant of The Heritage Institute.

An Eagle Scout, Perry attended National Camp School and served on his Local Council Camp Staff. As an adult, he has been a Scoutmaster, Blazer leader, and Troop Committee Chairman. Perry has also served on the Executive Board of the Ore-Ida Council.

Perry and his wife, Karen, have three daughters, two sons, and six grandchildren.

## Rod Zeeb

Rod Zeeb is the Co-Founder and CEO of The Heritage Institute, and co-developer of *The Heritage Process*.™ The Heritage Institute provides training in the discipline of Heritage Design, and professional certification in *The Heritage Process*.™ The Institute also conducts and distributes original research, offers mentoring, coaching and marketing support for professional advisors who wish to provide heritage planning to their constituents, and provides consulting services directly to individuals and families.

Through its affiliate, GenUs, the Institute also provides training in GenUs Design, which is the seamless integration of financial planning, estate planning and heritage design for clients. GenUs also provides training and coaching to professional advisors resulting in the profitable mindset of successful advisors and the alignment of excelling at what they enjoy.

Rod speaks nationally on issues related to *The Heritage Process*™, and is co-author of the novel, *What Matters*. Former Speaker of the House Newt Gingrich calls Rod "one of the leading players in economic thought in America" for his original contributions to the field of multi-generational planning.

Rod graduated Summa Cum Laude from Willamette College of Law in 1986, where he was Editor-in-Chief of the Willamette Law Review. He provides his time and expertise to many church, charitable, and community organizations, and enjoys travel, golf, and other activities with his children, Christina and Ryan, Ryan's wife, Kristin, and his grandchildren, Alexa, JD and Tyson.

# Looking out for the client (You!)

*Assembling a truly collaborative team of professionals*

One of life's undeniable truths is that there is no such thing as a smooth road to the future. The journey to the goals that matter most to you will be marked with twists and turns, and more than a few surprises. The professional advisor's role is to help you to discover the *outcomes* you want for yourself and for the people and communities about whom you care, and then to help you prepare for the journey—including all of those inevitable twists and turns.

Preparing and implementing all of the various plans, products, services and ongoing review and adjustment of your unique plan is a task that will ultimately be accomplished not by a single individual, but by a *team* of professionals from different disciplines. That team, with expertise in fields ranging from accounting and law to investing and insurance, will be an integral part not just of your planning, but in a very real sense, an integral part of your *life*.

For that reason, and since no matter where or with whom you do your planning in the future there will be some kind of professional advising team involved, we believe it's important for you to know how an effective **Collaborative Team Process** should function on your behalf. It's important that you understand how your team comes together, what it should look like, what you have the right to expect of them, how they can best work together to achieve your outcomes, and how you can fairly evaluate the team's performance.

### A lesson from baseball

Legendary major league baseball manager Casey Stengel once said, *"Finding good players is easy. Getting them to play together as a team is hard."* Professional advisors are like other people in that they come in all shapes, sizes, attitudes and competencies.

For our purpose here, let's assume that the pool of professionals from which you can select a team yourself, or potential team members who might be recommended by one of your trusted advisors, are all competent and experienced in their respective fields. That being the case, there are some important things for you to know about the team as it is assembled. For example, what are the characteristics of successful team players? What expectations should you have of the individual advisors, and of the team as a whole? What kinds of questions should you ask of them, and what performance hallmarks should you be able to observe that indicate that they are performing at a high level on your behalf?

### The team

Collaborative teams are made up of professional advisors from different disciplines. They are charged with important responsibilities on your behalf, including helping you to discover and clarify the outcomes you want in life—for *your* reasons! They must work together creatively, considering all of the alternatives available that can help to achieve the outcomes you want, and they must present those alternatives to you for your consideration.

After you have made your decisions from among the options presented, the team goes to work on implementation, ongoing review, administration and compliance to make sure the plan really will achieve the outcomes that you want.

Sounds pretty straightforward, right? And with the right team facilitator (or leader) it can be. But, a word of caution here: to paraphrase author Mark Twain, *"the difference between the team that's right for you and a team that's almost right is like the difference between lightning and the lightning bug."*

We believe that you should accept nothing less than the "lightning." Ever.

To achieve that level of performance requires an expert team facilitator. That they are the "leader," by the way, does not mean that they are necessarily your #1 trusted advisor. What it does mean is that they have the experience and ability to facilitate a process by which all of the team members align their talents and energies to form a true high-performance team dedicated to just one task: achieving your objectives.

A primary responsibility of the team facilitator is to promote positive, effective communication by encouraging strong interdependence among members of the team. This is done by creating and maintaining an atmosphere of equality, openness, positive intent, problem orientation and empathetic listening.

At the same time (this is the real world, after all) the team leader must discourage hidden agendas, inflated egos, competition, lack of trust and fear of failure. Your best outcomes in the planning and implementation process have a lot to do with how well your team is managed. (That's what our friend Casey Stengel was talking about earlier.)

### Getting to work for you

At the outset, the team leader will meet with each of the other advisors individually. At this meeting, the team leader will share your vision, and will provide the background behind its development. This is also an opportunity for the team leader to establish a personal relationship with that advisor if they haven't worked together before today.

When the entire team meets for the first time, the team leader knows that each of them understands not only your specific objectives, but also how and why they were developed. The first, and most important task, is to get the group to work collectively.

That can be a difficult job. For the group to accomplish its work, they must evolve from a collection of individuals, to a group, then to a team, and finally to a team operating in what can be called "the zone of inspiration," where a new synergy is achieved: a common focus on your objectives.

At the core of this team approach is the leader's responsibility to empower each member of the team to achieve your objectives. This is an important leadership principle. Each advisor/member of the team must be empowered sufficiently to recognize that the collective group will accomplish more than any advisor could by working individually.

When the right team comes together on your behalf at a high level of effective, interdependent communication and cooperation, they will display eight significant attributes as they move forward with their work. These attributes will be easy for you to observe and measure. In their work together, team members will display:

*True participative leadership.*

*Shared responsibility.*

*Purposeful alignment towards your objectives.*

*High communication.*

*Focus on the future.*

*Appreciation and utilization of creative talents.*

*Clear focus on the task at hand.*

*Rapid response.*

The truth is that effective and interdependent team collaboration of this kind is still a rare occurrence in the planning world. Communication between financial, legal and other professionals during the planning and implementation of most plans is typically achieved via e-mail, fax, phone and brief face-to-face meetings. That is not high-performance teamwork. And it is not what you have to accept.

You have a choice between lightning and the lightning bug. Prospective advisors who wish to work on your behalf (and be compensated for their services) should know where you stand on that choice from the outset.

In addition to specific attributes the team should display relative to their work with one another on your behalf, there are other key factors that you should expect from your team, and that you should be assured are taking place. They include:

**The team's acknowledgment that *you* are part of the team.** If this seems self-evident, please be aware that it isn't necessarily the case. You are more than the sum total of the data-sets that make up the financial, legal and insurance information that the team will review in order to make recommendations. You have a responsibility to see to it (where you feel it is appropriate) that the team is also aware of your values, ideals, life experiences, hopes, fears and dreams. A wise man once said that planning for the future of your family is not the same as planning for the future of your assets. Make sure that your team knows your "big picture."

**Your team communicates effectively with one another.** Each team member must know what is going on, and what progress is being made with implementation and ongoing reviews, administration and compliance. They must have a regular communication process, one that you play a role in.

**Your team understands what outcomes you want, and your** reasons for wanting those outcomes.

**Your team is creative and innovative** in seeking and considering options.

**Your team has other resources they can enlist** as temporary members when needed to deal with areas outside their areas of professional competency.

**Your team is clear about the expectations** they have of one another.

**Your team is clear about the expectations** that you have of them.

**Your team understands the importance of reviews**, administration and compliance to make sure the outcomes you desire are achieved.

## Making it happen

If this seems a daunting set of requirements for the team that you will eventually entrust with your planning, be assured that there are many professional advisors who are not only up to speed with the value and benefits of working in a high-performance team setting, but who prefer to work that way. They know that this is the best of all possible settings in which to achieve the outcomes their clients truly desire. It is also the venue within which they can bring their greatest professional strengths to the table—something that will benefit the team and you.

Keep the collaborative team process in mind as you select the advisors who will be responsible for protecting and providing for the people and organizations that matter most to you. Ask each potential advisor how they feel about the team process, and what their experience has been. Seek to distinguish between "lightning bug" style teamwork that is done remotely by e-mail and fax, and the "lightning" model, which is distinguished by face-to-face, high-performance focus and alignment in person. You might even share this article with your prospective advisors, and ask for their comments on the team process described here.

The road ahead is a winding one. That we cannot change. However, as you map out your route towards the outcomes that matter most to you, remember that the right team of professionals, working together in single-minded purpose on your behalf, can help you prepare for just about anything you'll face along your journey.

*(The authors are indebted to their associate Jack Beatty for his insights into the structure and function of truly collaborative professional teams.)*

## A Brief History of Estate Planning

*"The mouth of a perfectly contented man is filled with pure waters."*

With those words, the priest raised a jug of filtered water to the cloudless desert sky, then poured it out on top of the simple clay coffin. The water streamed across the terra-cotta lid, covered with a painted likeness of the coffin's occupant. Uah, sub-administrator in the corps of Sepdu, lord of the East, was ready for his final journey.

In ancient Egypt, the funeral of a government worker followed both law and custom, and the ceremonial pouring of clean water marked the close of the ritual. As soon as Uah's coffin was wedged into a small, nondescript tomb near the center of a vast complex of mud brick niches and burial vaults, his family gathered around a wooden table for the reading of his will.

The year was 1797 BC—over three thousand eight hundred years ago. In Uah's day, Egypt was tightly managed by a complex warren of civil law—much of it designed to protect private property. Estate planning customs and law had been around for many hundreds of years. When the priest read from the papyri will, he followed law that was already ancient when the first pyramids were built. Uah's assets were listed (except for his slaves—they were simply referred to as "those who live upon my land"), provisions made for his first and second wives, and agreements reached by his four children prior to his death were made a matter of public record. Finally, a certified copy of the will was signed by the priest, who would see that it was filed in the temple in accordance with Pharaoh's estate law decrees.

Historians agree that the story of mankind's social ascent from primitive savagery to civil (political) society is largely the story of private property; in particular, how that property was acquired, developed, and passed on to the next generation.

In early cultures, land was held in common, as a group or clan. Land that was productive for food and easy to defend was a precious commodity. So precious that the world's first armies evolved to protect property, not to spread political or religious systems. And, as the land they defended remained under the control of one clan for generations, the practice of doling out a small parcel to individuals within the group developed. Having fought—and sometimes died—for that land, the sense of personal ownership became a powerful cultural force.[1] As social organization grew more complex, and populations grew, it only made sense that parents pass along their hard won ground to their children. In a very real way, the absolute necessity for generally accepted rules of estate planning would become the catalyst for the emergence of civilization.

Over centuries, the crude wood and stone enclosures that protected clan groups of several dozen people grew into walled villages with hundreds of people, and the need to safeguard the inheritance of private property became increasingly important.

By the time Uah was being laid to rest in the Valley of the Nile, the people of ancient Mesopotamia were already living under the rule of the legal Code of King Hammurabi. Many of the Code's two hundred eighty-two laws dealt with economic issues, including estate planning.

---

1       Interestingly, the evolution of the idea of private property, and the right of inheritance existed in virtually every culture around the world thousands of years ago. Historian Louis H. Morgan points out that one enduring myth about Native Americans is that they had no private property, or only held land for the whole tribe. In fact, many tribes practiced individual ownership of property, and their laws for family succession and rules for selling lands were every bit as formal as those in Uah's Egypt.

BEATING THE MIDAS CURSE

That is a focus that has remained steady across millennia: in a recent survey of international legal systems done by the University of Chicago, it was reported that over seventy five percent of the laws on the books of any given nation dealt with property issues of one kind or another. King Hammurabi was truly ahead of his time.

For the classical Greeks, the concepts of the rule of law, and equality before the law, were based entirely on the primacy of protection of private property. Greek philosophers taught that private property was the wellspring from which all civilization developed, since by it man improved the soil, which provided for his family and strengthened his community.

(This is by no means a primitive or forgotten concept. Economist Murray N. Rothbard is in the mainstream of contemporary thinking when he says that, "all human rights are property rights." There can be no freedom of the press unless individuals are free to own printing presses, paper and ink. No freedom of speech unless an individual can own a hall or a radio station and invite anyone to speak on any topic. No freedom of religion unless individuals can build houses of worship. And all of these freedoms stem from the right to own and pass on property.)

Private property, and its transmission from generation to generation, was a deeply religious and cultural matter for the Greeks. They are credited as the first people to mark the boundaries of their property, which they did with small statues of household gods. The markers were a physical reflection of the family's daily prayer ritual. When a Greek asked a god to bless his land, he wanted the deity to know exactly where his land was! The Romans took a much more practical approach to property and estate planning. Under *Lex Romana*, property rights were legal, secular matters, not religious, as they had been under the Egyptians and Greeks. When Rome imposed order upon its far-flung empire, it was done with laws covering property and commerce as much as it was by the soldiers of their Legions.

Roman law covered all aspects of contracts, mortgages, credit and banking transactions, torts, fraud, insurance—even corporations and partnerships. And whatever else the conquered peoples of Europe and North Africa didn't like about their Roman masters, they knew a good thing when they saw it, and quickly adopted Roman law for their own purposes. In ancient Britain, for example, land had been held in common by tribes until the Roman conquest. After that, a Briton who became a Roman citizen acquired the right to private property, which under Roman law, was granted in perpetuity. The perpetual right to ownership was taken seriously; two thousand years after the Roman conquest, there are hundreds of British landholders who can trace their ownership directly back to land grants and purchase contracts made during the Roman occupation.

With the collapse of Rome in the fifth century AD, the empire fragmented into hundreds of small kingdoms and principalities. In recent years, historians have changed their minds about the commonly held view that this period should be called the "Dark Ages." In fact, from the fall of Rome to the blossoming of the Renaissance nine hundred years later, there continued to be a steady progression of innovative ideas and inventions in science, medicine, the arts and law. The end of the Empire did not mean everything Roman vanished from the face of the earth. Roman law remained the foundation of real estate and commercial transactions for over one thousand years.

, , ,

In medieval times, one Roman estate planning tradition took root more than any other. That was the concept of primogeniture, which could be summed up in five words: *the eldest son shall inherit.* Before there were wills, property passed down by "Canons of Descent" which promoted the ownership of the oldest son. Males were preferred over females and older children were preferred over younger children. Primogeniture was the norm throughout most of Western Europe, and eventually became part of English common law. It was a primary impetus for exploration and conquest (as second and third born sons struck out for the New World because they'd never inherit the family lands), and even for the creation of the first tax loopholes.

(As bad as primogeniture was, other cultures had some estate and inheritance situations that were worse. In medieval Japan, Samurai warriors who committed ritual suicide seldom did it to "save face." Usually it was for a much more practical reason: should they be executed for any reason, the law provided that their lands and possessions went to their master, they could not be passed on to their heirs. If they committed suicide after a death sentence was pronounced, however, their family was allowed to inherit the warrior's estate. )

Before the sixteenth century it was extremely difficult to bequeath land. In medieval Europe, estates were not thought of as relationships between people, as they are today, but as actual things in themselves. That meant the Crown was often in a position to sell an estate to the highest bidder, or give it to loyal followers. So a legal loophole was exploited by landowners by which the land was conveyed during the holder's lifetime to trustees *"to hold to the use of the owner's will."* The document instructing the trustees was known as his "Will".

Henry VIII, whose appetite for wives and fine food was exceeded only by his desire to acquire property and conduct war, wasn't about to allow the lawyers of the day to outmaneuver his tax code. As a way of ensuring a steady stream of revenue to his coffers, he strong-armed Parliament into the passage of the Statute of Uses, which closed the tax avoidance loopholes.

Then in 1540, Henry supported the passage of the Statute of Wills, which made the bequeathing of land legal. Landowners could divide it among their heirs, give it to charity, even disinherit their children altogether if they wished—as long as the Crown received its inheritance tax. Other property (money, furniture, tools, crops, leases, etc.) was transferable by means of a "Testament," and after 1540 the two documents were combined into one. Any male over the age of fourteen or female over the age of twelve (as long as she wasn't married—only a husband could approve of a wife's will) could make a valid will that planned for the passing of his or her estate.

The Statute of Wills governed estate planning in England—and soon most of Europe—until 1837. In fact, parts of the original Statute were still in use in Scotland until 1926. (In particular the prohibition against prisoners, lunatics or traitors being able to leave valid wills.)

, , ,

Primogeniture, and the entire body of English Common law, accompanied the first settlers to the shores of America. But in the colonies, inheritance laws, like many European traditions, soon fell by the wayside. America had vast expanses of land that anyone could lay claim to (particularly as the native tribes were pushed further east and south), and as for the importance of family connections, the custom in colonial America was that if a man didn't volunteer his history, you didn't ask. The old rules of class-conscious medieval Europe didn't work in a place where a man could prosper through his own hard work and enterprise—no matter who his parents had been.

One of the differences between the American colonies and, say, the one-time penal colony of Australia was that America was settled by such a wide variety of peoples; in the pubs of Boston and Philadelphia, indentured servants and debtors rubbed shoulders with the second and third sons of landed gentry who had been excluded from significant inheritances by old world custom.

America offered a level playing field to all who wished to work and dream and sacrifice. In itself, this was a revolutionary condition. No society in history since the earliest hunter-gatherers had done so.

Primogeniture did prevail for some time in the southern colonies. With their large plantations, and slave-dependent economy, southern landowners struggled to retain the trappings of the English upper class. In the middle and northern colonies, however, the reality of hard-scrabble life on the rugged frontier brought huge changes in the established social structure.

As Governor Talcott of Connecticut said in 1699, "Much of our land remains un-subdued, and will remain so without the assistance of younger sons, which in reason can't be expected if they will have no part of the inheritance." So, a "multigeniture" system quickly became the norm in the northern and middle colonies.

Thomas Jefferson believed that to own land and to make it productive was the birthright of every American. He also had his own strong feelings about traditional estate planning of the time that favored giving the eldest son a "double-portion" of the estate. "If he could eat twice as much or do double the work," it might be evidence of his right to a double portion of the estate. However, to Jefferson, the eldest son was "on a par in his powers and his wants" with his siblings, and so he concluded that equal inheritance was the preferable system.

, , ,

In many ways the history of estate planning has been the history of taxation. That has been the case in the United States since the first federal estate tax was passed in 1797. From that day to ours, estate taxes have been applied, then rescinded, and applied again, as regularly as the changing tides. Funding wars, social programs, highway programs—the need for a constant flow (some would say torrent) of monies into the federal treasury has never declined. Estate taxation has always been an apple literally waiting to drop into the tax collector's outstretched hand.

In American history, the imposition of new estate taxes have often coincided with efforts to improve the national balance sheet in a time of military or social crisis. In 1797, when a blockade by the French navy threatened to wipe out trans-Atlantic trade, Congress passed the Stamp Act, which required citizens to purchase federal stamps on wills and other inheritance documents. This first estate tax raised funds to re-build the navy, and was repealed in 1802.

The first direct tax on inheritances came during the Civil War, with the passage of the Revenue Act of 1862. Blood relatives—other than spouses—receiving inheritances of more than $1,000 were required to pay a three-fourths of one percent tax. (It rose to five percent on gifts to more distant relatives or strangers.) In 1864, the top rate was raised to six percent. This tax was repealed in 1870.

The U.S. went to war again in 1898 war after the sinking of the battleship *Maine* in Cuba. To fund this war, Congress passed the War Revenue Act of 1898, which imposed taxes on both estates *and* gifts. Rates rose (after an exemption of $10,000) from three-fourths of one percent up to fifteen percent on estates over $1 million. Like its predecessors, this tax had a relatively short life, and was repealed in 1902.

Congress passed the Revenue Act of 1916 as America prepared to enter World War I. It levied taxes of from one percent after a $50,000 exemption—up to ten percent for estates valued at over $5 million. In 1917, the top rate was increased to twenty-five percent on estates above $10 million. Then in 1926, the estate tax was reduced, but, by this time, the notion of government ever turning its back on the estate tax gift horse looked increasingly unlikely.

Franklin Roosevelt turned to the estate tax to help fund New Deal programs. In 1932, the gift tax that had been abolished in 1924, was reinstated, and in 1934, the estate tax was increased to sixty percent for estates greater than $10 million. Unlike the repeals following other wars, the estate tax was not abolished after World War II. It was then, and remains today, a small part of overall federal revenues—about one and one-half percent, but in the days of trillion-dollar budgets, it still has an impact.

For most of the last five hundred years, people have looked at the estate planning process primarily from a tax perspective. The quest to minimize what one poet called *"a man's final and most humiliating tithe,"* has dominated the process for so long, and with such complete effect, that for many it is hard to conceive of a world without a death tax.

Presently, the reality of the estate tax is still the eight hundred pound gorilla of the financial planning process. The response by financial and legal advisors to the last grab of the tax collector's hand into their client's pockets as the coffin lid is being closed has been to develop a wide array of products and strategies to keep the pain of the last tax bite to a minimum. And they've done a very good job providing that protection. Yet, by making the main focus of the estate planning process minimization of taxes, traditional advisors may have helped open a Pandora's box. These unanticipated problems have, over the years, destroyed more families, and more fortunes, than any estate tax in history.

Those problems, and their solutions, are the focus of this book. They can be traced back thousands of years, to the first primitive landholder who ever fought off marauding neighbors so that he could lay claim to a small patch of fertile, defendable land.

Who would inherit the land when he no longer had the strength to lead the clan? What would his children, and their children, make of the gifts that their parents would pass to them? Would they really ever understand the sacrifice that went into making the land valuable? Would they instruct their own children the way they had been taught? Would they appreciate, respect and apply the lessons their parents had worked diligently to instill within them?

Thousands of years ago those questions haunted every parent who owned property and understood the absolute limits imposed by their mortality. We ask similar questions today, updated and modernized to be sure, but more like our ancestors' questions than we probably realize.

*Heritage design answers those questions.*

, , ,

.

# List of Illustrations

Cover Design: Brad Haga
90% World: Jackson Pollack, *Untitled,* 1948
King Midas: University of Athens Collection
Chapter 1: Marianne Strait, *Victorian Collection*
Chapter 2: Bank of England, *A History*
Chapter 3: Cornelius Vanderbilt, Vanderbilt University
Chapter 4: Thad Blake, *Message in a Bottle*
Chapter 5: R. Dowan, *Forest Dark*
Chapter 6: Douglas Haga, *Lopez Island*
Chapter 7: Douglas Haga, *Siletz River-Clouds & Wind*
Chapter 8: Douglas Haga, *Bay Road Egret*
Chapter 9: Asher Durand, *Genesee Valley Landscape,* 1853
Chapter 10: Douglas Haga, *Seal Rock Series #12*
Chapter 11: Thomas Cole, *The Oxbow,* 1836
Chapter 12: Douglas Haga, *Bay Road #4*
Chapter 13: George Cole, *Harvest,* 1865
Chapter 14: N.C. Wyeth, *Captain John Paul Jones,* 1939

Appendix
Illustrations: Statler Cowe, *The Race*
Cairo Musem, *Panel from Tomb of Hatshepsut*

# Selected Bibliography

Allen-Burley, Madelyn. *Listening.* New York, NY: John Wiley & Sons, Inc., 1995.

Allport, Gordon, W.P.E. Vernon and Garnder Lindzey. *Study of Values.* Boston: Houghton, Mifflin, 1960.

Anderson, J.R. *Learning and Memory.* New York: Wiley, 1995.

Atkinson, J.W. and D. Birch. *Introduction to Motivation* (2nd ed.). New York: Wiley, Van Nostrand, 1978.

Atkinson, R.K., S.J. Derry, A. Renkl and D. Worham. *Learning from examples: instructional principles from the worked examples research.* Review of Educational Research, 70, 181-214 (2000).

Avery, Robert B. and Michael S. Rendall. *Estimating the size and distribution of baby boomers' prospective inheritances.* Cornell University for Presentation at the Philanthropy Roundtable, (Nov. 11, 1993).

Avery, Robert B. and Michael S. Rendall. *Inheritance and wealth.* Cornell University For Presentation at the Philanthropy Roundtable, (Nov. 11,1993). "The Cornell Study."

Bernstein, William J. *The Birth of Plenty.* New York, NY: McGraw-Hill Publishing, 2004.

Bower, G.H. *The Nature of Emotion.* New York: Oxford University Press, 1994. Some relations between emotions and memory. In P. Ekman and R.J. Davidson (Eds.).

Boyack, Merrilee Brown. *The Parenting Breakthrough.* Salt Lake City, UT: Deseret Book Company, 2005.

Boyatzis, Richard E., Angela J. Murphy and Jane V. Wheeler. *Philosophy as a missing link between values and behavior.* Psychological Reports, 86, 47-64 (2000).

Bradley, Susan and Mary Martin. *Sudden Money.* New York, NY: John

Wiley & Sons Inc., 2002.

Bradshaw, John. *The Family.* Deerfield Beach, Florida: Health Communications, Inc, 1998.

Bragstad, B.J. and S.M. Stumpf. *A Guidebook for Teaching Study Skills and Motivation.* Boston: Allyn & Bacon, 1982.

Brancaccio, David. *Squandering Aimlessly.* New York, NY: Simon & Schuster, 2000.

Bransford, J.D., J.J. Franks, N.J.Vye and R.D. Sherwood. *Similarity and Analogical Reasoning.* Cambridge, England: Cambridge University Press, 1989, pp. 470-497. New approaches to instruction: because wisdom can't be told. In S.Vosniadou & A. Ortony (Eds.).

Brickman, S., R.B. Miller and T.D. Roedel. *Goal valuing and future consequences as predictors of cognitive engagement.* Paper presented at the annual meeting of the American Educational Research Association, Chicago (March 1997).

Brill, Marla. *Windfall.* Indianapolis, IN: ALPHA, 2002.

Brinkman, Rick and Rick Kirschner. *Dealing with Relatives.* New York, NY: McGraw-Hill, 2003.

Broadbent, D.E. *Perception and Communication.* London: Pergamon Press, 1958.

Brooks, Andree Aelion. *Children of Fast-Track Parents.* New York, NY: Penguin Group, 1989.

Brooks, David. *Bobos In Paradise.* New York, NY: Simon & Schuster, 2000.

Brophy, J.E. and J. Alleman. *Advances in Research on Teaching.* Greenwich, CT: JAI Press, 1992.

Bruner, J.S. *The act of discovery.* Harvard Educational Review, 31, 21-32 (1961).

Burley-Allen, Madelyn. *Listening: The Forgotten Skill.* Canada: John Wiley & Sons, Inc., 1995.

Butler, D.L. and P.H. Winne. *Feedback and self-regulated learning: a theoretical synthesis.* Review of Educational Research, 65, 245-281 (1995).

B.Z. Posner and W.H. Schmidt. *Values congruence and differences between and interplay of personal and organizational value systems.* Journal of Business Ethics, 12, 171-177 (1993).

Callahan, Sidney Cornelia. *Parents Forever.* New York: Crossroads Publishing Co., 1992.

Card, Emily W. and Adam L. Miller. *Managing Your Inheritance.* New York: Times Books, 1996.

Carroll, Lenedra J. *The Architecture of All Abundance.* Novato, CA: New World Library, 2001.

Christiansen, Tim and Sharon A. DeVaney. *Antecedents of trust and commitment in the financial planner-client relationship.* Association for Financial Counseling and Planning Education, (1998).

Ciaramicoli, Arthur and Katherine Ketcham. *The Power of Empathy.* New York: Dutton, 2000.

Cleary, Thomas. *The Art of Wealth.* Deerfield Beach, FL: Health Communications, 1998.

Coles, Robert. *Privileged Ones.* Boston: Little, Brown & Company, 1977.

Collier, Charles W. *Wealth in Families.* Published by Harvard University, 2002.

*Communicating more effectively with older clients.* Trusts & Estates, p. 58 (April 2000).

*Controlling behavior by controlling the inheritance.* Probate & Property, p. 6 (Sept/Oct)

Crawford, Tad. *The Secret Life of Money.* New York: G.P. Putnam's Sons, 1994.

Cutler, Neal E. *Advising Mature Clients.* New York: John Wiley & Sons Inc.,

2002.

D'Souza, Dinesh. *The Virtue of Prosperity.* New York: NY: TouchStone, 2000.

Dalphonse, Sherri. *Love and money.* Washington, 48 (Feb 2000).

Damon, William. *The Moral Child.* New York: The Free Press, 1988.

Davis, Ken and Tom Taylor. *Kids and Cash.* La Jolla, CA: Oak Tree Publications, Inc., 1979.

DeGraaf, John, David Wann and Thomas H. Naylor. *Affluenza.* San Francisco, CA: Berrett-Koehler Publishers, Inc., 2001.

Dominguez, Joe and Vicki Robin. *Your Money or Your Life.* New York: Penguin, 1992, xx.

Domini, Amy L., Dennis Pearne and Sharon L. Rich. *The Challenges of Wealth.* Homewood, IL: Dow Jones-Irwin, 1998.

DuFour, Richard and Robert Eaker. *Professional Learning Communities at Work.* Bloomington, IN: National Educational Service, 1998.

Easterbrook, Gregg. *The Progress Paradox.* New York: Random House Trade Paperbacks, 2004.

Edelman, Ric. *Ordinary People, Extraordinary Wealth.* New York, NY: HarperCollins, 2000.

Erikson, Joan M. *The Life Cycle Completed.* New York, NY: W.W. Norton & Company, 1997.

Eyre, Linda & Richard. *Teaching Your Children Values.* New York, NY: Fireside, 1993.

Fish, Barry, Les Kotzer. *The Family Fight.* Washington D.C.: Continental Atlantic Publications Inc., 2002.

Fisher, Marc. *Naming your price-many Americans find that the money they desire is never quite enough.* Washington Post, C1 (June 30, 1997).

Ford, M.E. *Motivating Humans.* Newbury Park, CA: Sage, 1992.

Forward, Susan, and Craig Buck. *Toxic Parents.* New York: Bantam Books, 1989.

Frank, Robert. *Luxury Fever.* New York, NY: The Free Press, 1999.

Gagnier, Regenia. *The Insatiability of Human Wants.* Chicago, IL: The University of Chicago Press, 2000.

Gallo, Eileen and John Gallo. *Silver Spoon Kids.* New York, NY: Contemporary Books, 2002.

Gardner, Howard. *Changing Minds.* Boston, MA: Harvard Business School Press, 2004.

Gates, William H., Sr., and Chuck Collins. *Wealth and Our Common Wealth.* Boston, MA: Beacon Press, 2002.

Gilbert, Roberta M. *Extraordinary Relationships.* New York: John Wiley, 1992.

Glaser, R. *Cognitive Functioning and Social Structure over the Life Course.* Norwood, NJ: Ablex, 1987.

Grant, James. *The Trouble with Prosperity.* New York: Times Books, 1996.

Gurney, Kathleen. *Knowing your money personality can help you find the right financial advisor for you.* Financial Psychology Corporation, (1999).

Gutherie, E.R. *The Psychology of Learning.* New York: Harper & Row, 1935.
Hall, J.F. *The Psychology of Learning.* Philadelphia: J.B. Lippincott, 1966.

Handy, Charles. *The Age of Paradox.* Boston, Massachusetts: Harvard Business School Press, 1994.

Hausner, Lee. *Children of Paradise.* Los Angeles, CA: Jeremy P. Tarcher, 1990.

Hayes, Christopher L. *What's your money personality?* Working Woman, 35 (Feb 1995).

Hetcher, Michael, Lynn Nadel, and Richard E. Michod, eds. *The Origin of Values.* New York: Aldine de Gruyter, 1993. p. 1-28.

Hoffman, M.L. *Moral Behavior and Development.* Hillsdale, NJ: Erlbaum, 1991.

*Empathy, social cognition, and moral action.* In W.M. Kurtines & J.L. Gewirtz (Eds.).

Hughes, James E., Jr. *Family Wealth.* Princeton Junction, NJ: NetWrx, Inc., 1997.

*Interviewing the affluent: unpacking philanthropic values and motivations."* 11th National Conference on Planned Giving, (Oct 9, 1998).

Jones, Laurie Beth. *The Path.* New York, NY: Tyndale House Publishers, 1971.

Kinder, George. *The Seven Stages of Money Maturity.* New York, NY: Dell Publishing, 1997.

Kleberg, Sally S. *The Stewardship of Private Wealth.* NY: McGraw-Hill, 1997.

Klingelhofer, Edwin L. *Coping with Your Grown Children.* Clifton, NJ: Humana Press, 1989.

Kluckhohn, Florence and Fred Strodtbeck. *Variations in Value Orientations.* Evanston, IL: Row, Peterson & Co, 1961.

Kohn, Alfie. *Punished by Rewards.* New York: Houghton Mifflin Co., 1999.

Kotre, John PH.D. *Make it Count.* NY, NY: The Free Press, 1999.

Lave, J., and E. Wenger E. *Situated Learning.* Cambridge, England: Cambridge University Press, 1991.

Lennick, Doug and Fred Kiel. *Moral Intelligence.* Upper Saddle River, NJ: Wharton School Publishing, 2005.

Linder, Ray. *What Will I Do with My Money?* Chicago, IL: Northfield Publishing, 2000.

Link, E.G. and Peter Tedstrom. *Getting to the Heart of the Matter.* Franklin, Indiana: Professional Mentoring Program, 1999.

M. Rokeach, *The Nature of Human Values.* New York: Free Press, 1973.

Martin, V.L. and M. Pressley. *Elaborative-interrogation effects depend on the nature of the question.* Journal of Educational Psychology, 83, 113–119 (1991).

Massialas, B.G. and J. Zevin. *Teaching Creatively: Learning through Discovery.* Malabar, FL: Robert F. Krieger, 1983.

McAleese, Tama. *Money Power for Families.* Hawthorne, NJ: The Career Press, 1993.

McBride, Tracey. *Frugal Luxuries.* New York: Bantam Books, 1997.

McInerney, Francis and Sean White. *Future Wealth.* New York: St. Martin's Press, 2000.

Mellan, Olivia. *Money Harmony.* New York: Walker and Company, 1994.

Needleman, Jacob. *Money and the Meaning of Life.* New York: Doubleday, 1991.

Nemeth, Maria. *The Energy of Money.* New York: Ballantine Publishing Group, 1997.

Morris, P. *Adult Learning.* London: Wiley, 1977.

Nichols, Michael P. *The Lost Art of Listening.* New York, NY: The Guilford Press, 1995.

Olsen, Timothy. *The Teenage Investor.* NY: McGraw-Hill, 2003.

Patterson, Kerry, Joseph Grenny, Ron McMillian, and Al Switzler. *Crucial Conversations.* New York, NY. McGraw-Hill, 2002.

Pearl, Jayne A. *Kids and Money.* Princeton, NJ: Bloomberg Press, 1999.

Potter, Peter. *All About Money.* New Canaan, CT: William Mulvey, Inc., 1988.

Price, Deborah L. *Money Therapy.* Novato, CA: New World Library, 2000.

Prince, Russ Alan and Karen Maru File. *The Seven Faces of Philanthropy.* San Francisco, CA: Jossey-Bass Publishers, 1994.

*Raising a responsible child of wealth.* Trusts & Estates, p. 42 (June 2001).

*Restraining on inheritance can accomplish a client's objectives.* Estate
      Planning, p. 124 (March 2003).

Rosenberg, Claude Jr. *Wealthy and Wise.* Canada: Little, Brown & Company
      Limited, 1994.

Rottenberg, Dan. *The Inheritor's Handbook.* New York, NY: Fireside, 1999.

Russell, Bob. *Money.* Sisters, OR: Multnomah Books, 1977.

Schervish, P.G. *Philanthropy among the wealthy: empowerment, motivation,
and strategy.* Paper presented on the Rocky Mountain Philanthropic
Institute, Vail, CO, (July 1991).

Schwartz, Shalom H. *Universals in the content and structure of value:
      theoretical advances and empirical tests in 20 countries.* Advances in
      Experimental Social Psychology. NY: Academic Press, 5, 1-65 (1992).

Sedgwich, John. *Rich Kids.* New York: William Morrow, 1972.

Shore, Bill. *The Cathedral Within.* New York: Random House, 1999.

Solomon, Robert J. *When are unequal bequests to children equitable?* Estate
      Planning, 139 (March 2004).

Spence, Linda. *Legacy.* Athens, OH: Swallow Press, 1977.

Stanley, Thomas. *Marketing to the Affluent.* New York: McGraw-Hill, 1988.

Stanley, Thomas J. *The Millionaire Mind.* Kansas City, MO: Andrew
McMeel Publishing, 2000.

Steiger, Heidi L. *Wealthy & Wise.* Hoboken, New Jersey: John Wiley & Sons,
      2003.
Thornton, Cameron and Rod Zeeb: *What Matters,* Heritage Institute Press, 2012

Twist, Lynne. *The Soul of Money: Transforming.* New York: W.W.
      Norton & Company, 2003.

Vitt, Lois, Carol Anderson, Jamie Kent, Danna M. Lyter,
Jurg K. Siegenthaler, and Jeremy Ward. *Personal finance and the
rush to competence: financial literacy education in the U.S.* A Study
Conducted by: The Institute of Socio-Financial Studies for the
Fannie Mae Foundation, (2000).
Williams, Roy & Vic Preisser. *Philanthropy Heirs & Values.* Bandon, OR:
Robert D. Reed Publishers, 2005.

Willis, Thayer Cheatham. *Navigating the Dark Side of Wealth.* Portland, OR:
New Concord Press, 2003.

Wixon, Burton N. *Children of the Rich.* New York: Crown, 1973.

Woloshyn, V.E., M. Pressley and W. Schneider. *Elaborative-interrogation
and prior knowledge effects on learning of facts.* Journal of
Educational Psychology, 84, 115-124 (1992).

Wong, B.Y.L. *Self-questioning instructional research: a review.* Review
of Educational Research, 55, 227-268 (1985).

Zelizer, Viviana A. *The Social Meaning of Money.* New York, NY:
BasicBooks, 1994.

Zimmerman, Stuart and Jared Rosen. *Inner Security & Infinite Wealth.* NY:
SelectBooks Inc., 2003.

# INDEX

GenUs LLC
701 North Green Valley Parkway, Suite 200,
Henderson, Nevada, 89074
*info@genusu.com*

CPSIA information can be obtained at www.ICGtesting.com
Printed in the USA
LVOW10s1921161015

458598LV00002B/61/P

9 781494 735456